THE QUEST FOR MASTERY

WITHDRAWN

The Quest for Mastery

Positive Youth Development Through Out-of-School Programs

SAM M. INTRATOR
DON SIEGEL

Harvard Education Press
Cambridge, Massachusetts

KH

Library of Congress Control Number 2013951065

Paperback ISBN 978-1-61250-659-3
Library Edition ISBN 978-1-61250-660-9

Published by Harvard Education Press,
an imprint of the Harvard Education Publishing Group

Harvard Education Press
8 Story Street
Cambridge, MA 02138

Cover Design: Ciano Design
Cover Photos: © Gabriel Amadeus Cooney
The typefaces used in this book are Adobe Garamond Pro, Futura, and Indispose

9/30/15

The poet Percy Bysshe Shelley wrote, "The great instrument of moral good is the imagination." This book is dedicated to the bold and imaginative women and men who started the programs we examined with just a small and fledgling idea and virtually no support or resources. From these humble beginnings, they worked with colleagues, volunteers, advisors, and funders to build programs that strive toward the "moral good" of leveling the playing field between underserved youth and their more advantaged peers.

CONTENTS

Imagine if President Bill Clinton took on a gig as the basketball coach of fourth graders at a local YMCA. You can imagine him lighting up the sideline: animated, enthusiastic, and fully absorbed in managing his players and the game. In the early years of Project Coach, we had a young man in the program whose charisma and energy were Clintonesque. His name was Luis,[1] and the elementary-aged children would listen to him spellbound by the special alchemic mix of inspiration, ferocity, and intensity. Luis was just fifteen, but he would work the sideline, exhorting kids to hustle, pass the ball, and play defense, and when one of his little hoopsters made a good play he would emote passionate and contagious joy.

One of our favorite recollections is watching little hoop players clamber around him during an end-of-game huddle. The "huddles" function as opportunities for our teenage coaches to teach about values, character, and the ways lessons learned by playing sports apply to life and school. He asked, "How do you show that you are trying hard on the court?" His purple-clad team chimed in with answers like "You run hard," "You cheer with a loud voice for your teammates," and "You sweat a lot!" After they brainstormed, he changed the question to "How do you show that you are trying hard in the classroom?" It was beautiful to watch. In sports, they call promising athletes "blue-chip" prospects (the blue refers to poker, where the highest-valued chip is blue). Luis was a blue-chip prospect, but . . .

But we lost him after two years. Apparently his "talent" also appealed to the ubiquitous gangs of Springfield. His special mix of interpersonal qualities and pulsating intensity served him well not only in the gym, but also in the neighborhood and in school. His decline in program participation occurred sporadically, in fits and starts. We tried to keep him involved, but the gravitational pull of the gangs gradually drew him from our orbit. We actively tried to intervene. We helped him get into family therapy. We reached out to counselors who specialized in at-risk boys and we reached out to the schools. Each attempt worked, but only for a short time. We started to see him less often in the program, and then he stopped coming altogether.

Luis spent twenty-seven months in prison awaiting trial after being charged for an execution-style gang murder. In the years that we worked with him, we sensed that he was constantly teetering on a narrow ledge. On one side, there was our program, school, and the conventional road to a positive future. The other side of the ridge was the foreboding terrain of Springfield's streets. In writing this book, we thought of Luis all the time.

WRITING A BOOK IS AN exercise in expressing your expertise. Readers assume that the authors have studied the problem and mapped out a coherent solution. We have strived to do this, but we wrote this book while simultaneously enmeshed in our youth program. To work in the lives of low-income teenagers who are growing up in neighborhoods plagued by violence, underemployment, and gangs is a humbling experience. The daily grind and challenge of their lives provides an unequivocal dose of humility. Project Coach and all the programs we visited represent herculean efforts on the part of well-meaning adults to provide a structure and a safe space for these young people to grow up. The energy and ingenuity of the staff who opened their lives and programs to us was inspiring and compelling. This book is our effort to tell the story of these programs and to provide a map of this burgeoning field. Yet, every program has multiple stories like the one of our blue-chip coach.

What we can say is that good programs possess a capacity for connectedness. They weave a complex web of relationships among the staff, the youth, the activity they focus on, and the various contexts in the lives of young people: school, family, peers, and neighborhood. These webs are intricate, fragile, and woven by a wide array of methods, from mentoring, apprenticeships, formal classes, problem-based learning, and collaboration to athletics, art, music, travel, and more. The complexity of the relationships means that young people often find a space and a connection that works in transformative ways, but it also means that other youth slip through the web. In the end, the work is deeply humbling, occasionally triumphant, and sometimes full of poignant high-stakes failure. This book acknowledges all of these outcomes, because we have lived every ebb and flow and have had our hearts both lifted and broken by this work.

As we were finishing the book, Luis was acquitted; he had spent over two years of his adolescence in prison. Days after being released, he called us. He is now nineteen and is planning to attend college. He told us, "I had a lot of time to think and I want to come back. Project Coach was the best thing I did when I was growing up and I want that life back." The programs we describe strive to be powerful assets for youth. It is hard work, but some formidable magic lives in these organizations. This is our effort to tell their story.

—Sam Intrator and Don Siegel
Northampton, Massachusetts

"Everything and the Kitchen Sink"

"Lacrosse saved my life," said the young woman with a shock of unruly black hair, her eyes downcast. "I don't play lacrosse anymore, and I barely played in high school, but if it wasn't for MetroLacrosse, I think I would be back in Charlestown, maybe in jail, maybe pregnant, and probably doing things that would be bad—really bad for me."

The first day of an upper-level seminar in a college classroom rarely produces much in the way of drama. There might be the occasional moment of intellectual electricity, but mostly the undergraduates and professors know the drill and efficiently wend their way through the rituals of covering the syllabus and the details of the upcoming semester. This young woman's sharing caused quite a stir, as everyone in the room swiveled to look intently at her, but it also became the inspiration for this book and for nearly ten years of work with underserved youth.

We co-teach a class at Smith College titled Urban Educational Policy. Once students settle in, we begin by asking them to introduce themselves to their fellow students and to us by explaining their path to higher education. We offer some prompts and then give them a few minutes to jot down their thoughts on these questions: Who influenced you? What explains why you are here in this room and not somewhere else? What people were part of the team that shaped the trajectory of your journey? What activities were significant to your development as you moved through your adolescence?

Their introductions typically fall into one of three basic variations that capture the conventional sociocultural analyses of education: Schooling fits into a larger framework of society. The dynamics and systems of economics, politics, and culture interact in predictable ways. As this is a highly competitive and top-ranked liberal arts college, the first and most common narrative speaks to what might be thought of as the "hard work" theme. This view contends that success is based on a recipe of industriousness, sustained focus, individual merit, and ambition. School—like society—is a place where individuals prove their worth and capacity by hard work that develops a student's capacities. An introduction in this mode would resemble the following:

> I went to a big public suburban high school. I was in honors and advanced placement classes and I worked my tail off. In my junior year I took six AP classes, served as junior class vice-president, sang in the Glee Club, and worked at the mall. It was intense but I got through the race, as did most of my friends.

A second variation acknowledges how class and cultural capital function to effectively pass knowledge, skills, capacities, and aspirations from one generation to the next. These narratives recognize the incontrovertible link between a child's educational and academic performance and a family's educational background. A narrative in this spirit might begin like this:

> I grew up outside of Boston and attended public school, where I played sports and the piano. Education and learning was deeply valued in our family and my mother, who is a Smith alumna, would bring me back to Northampton once every few years to visit Smith.

A third form of introduction offers homage to "strong schooling." These students grew up in modest or poor urban neighborhoods and describe attending mission-driven schools that were fervidly intent on providing academic experiences that closed the achievement gap.

> I attended a charter school in Boston and we went to school from 8:30 to 5:30 every day. We didn't really have sports because we were a small charter school. We had academics and then occasional trips or other school-related activities in the afternoons. My teachers and counselors pushed us every day toward college. It was intense and highly structured. We visited colleges starting in ninth grade and we had all sorts of systems for teaching us how to get through the applications. All the teachers and administrators were focused on this all the time. I was really close to my teachers because they worked with us in something called advisory and we were together for so many years.

Sprinkled among these is a distinctly different variation. If the first three narratives are like progressing through the FM dial and hearing jazz, classic rock, then pop, the fourth is like energetic rap. It grabs your attention with its pulsing and edgy sound. These narratives resemble the "Lacrosse saved my life" motif.

> I hated school. I was a terrible student and my school was horrible, but I had a friend who got me involved in this program and I started doing metal work and sculpture. I spent every day in the studio and I met Bob and Kathy and I learned how to make art and they helped me get on and sort of stay on the straight path in school.

One particularly vivid story illuminated how these programs were floating out there without much publicity or recognition. Young people didn't go looking for these programs but bumped into them by happenstance.

> One day in middle school, I walked past this lady in the lunchroom. She had this machine, which looked weird, and I walked past her. She called over to me and I turned back. I don't know why I did.

This machine was an erg [a rowing ergometer used for indoor train-ing]. I got on and rowed for about a minute and she said, "You can be good." I sometimes think that I never would be here at Smith—a Haitian woman from a poor family who went to bad schools—if I didn't turn back and get on that erg. I don't row anymore, but it got me here because it gave me a family that taught me things and helped me with school and then helped me figure out how to get to and pay for college.

Another student described how, in eighth grade, she bumped into an elementary school teacher who said, "I remember you liked music. I have a friend working at a program. Let me take you down to meet her."

These narratives seized our attention. They described something alive and emergent at work that was not described in the journals or reports about urban educational reform. Part of the appeal to us was that the programs represented a radical departure from the approach dominating policy and practice in American education, which narrowly emphasizes lit-eracy and numeracy skills. Instead, these programs took a more expansive view of what it meant to help children flourish; they focused on building core capacities and character attributes through high-interest and engag-ing activities. These programs appeared to heed Plutarch's maxim, "The mind is not a vessel to be filled but a fire to be kindled." They took seri-ously the need for youth to find inspiration and excitement in their work and learning.

In our interviews with youth and young adults, we repeatedly heard that the school experience is dry, wooden, and disconnected from their present lives and sense of the future. Such testimonials are reflected in their grades, standardized test scores, and dismal graduation rates. When we venture into some of these schools we immediately get a feeling that their central role is one of social and physical control, more than of spark-ing curiosity, excitement for learning, and critical thinking. Yet, when we see the same kids in the context of out-of-school programs, we see a mirror image. They are fully engaged and "firing on all cylinders." Moreover, they are acquiring an array of assets that we believe are truly transformative, and responsible for the "lacrosse saved my life" narrative that we have come to hear over the years in one form or another.

The programs that we portray in this book have developed curricula, pedagogies, and practices that explicitly teach critical attitudes, emotional regulation skills, and social values in ways that fit naturally into kids' lives. While participating in activities such as playing lacrosse or creating art, youth learn to set and realize goals, problem solve when things go awry, focus their attention and regulate their emotions, persevere when encountering adversity, communicate with diverse people in different settings, take responsibility for their actions, and value prosocial norms of behavior. Ultimately, these organizations develop youth who are dynamic, creative, and resilient and who can become assets to their community, prized by their families, and successful as students. Critical to such development is their unyielding commitment to keep participants "on the rails" and to provide whatever support is necessary to make certain that kids thrive despite the many challenges encountered today in underserved communities.

Our journey into this world brought us into contact with wonderful and inspiring people. We visited imaginative and innovative programs that are helping youth transform their lives. Practitioners proudly gave us tours and described the development of their distinctive approach to supporting and educating children. We watched young people build things, serve their communities, negotiate with each other, create beautiful art, play, and more.

A director of one of the programs we visited told us, "We get to know our kids and then we do whatever they need. We do everything we can." This is the story of a set of programs that routinely strive to "throw everything and the kitchen sink" at the intractable problem of helping high-need but promising young people fulfill the American dream. The "everything and the kitchen sink" theme reflects the idea that great programs, like good parents, must be responsive to what their kids need to best move youth along a positive trajectory. In researching this book, we heard this theme reiterated countless times in one form or another. In essence, great programs complement and supplement the work of parents and schools in helping to cultivate the knowledge, skills, values, and resources necessary for all youth to compete on a more level playing field and to pursue their dreams.

OUR INITIAL FORAYS INTO LEARNING ABOUT YOUTH DEVELOPMENT PROGRAMS

We were drawn to learn more about the out-of-school programs that our students described as influential, even pivotal, in their life and development. We began doing some in-depth interviews with our students—both informally and formally. What were the programs that these college students attended? How and why did these programs have such a seemingly powerful influence on how teenagers thought about themselves and their aspirations? What processes did the programs use to shape young people?

One of the recurring themes was fascinating, troubling, and counterintuitive to the educational policy talk that dominated the field. The young people we talked with often described how they made it to college despite attending schools they considered "poor" or "not challenging." A fairly typical story from Natasha, a young woman, captures the tension. She attended high school in Los Angeles, and after a discussion about the role that out-of-school programs could play in the lives of urban youth, she wrote this note:

> It is difficult for me to talk about my experience in high school; it brings me back to a place I fought so hard to get away from. The demographics of my high school . . . consisted of students from poor and working class families, about two percent White, and the rest were mostly African American and Hispanics. I was one of the few students trying to crawl out of the barrel, while being pushed down by the forces of my school and my community. I did not have friends who went to "better" schools for me to compare myself with academically. However, during my junior year, my guidance counselor advised me to join a program outside the school . . . because my school was not challenging me.

It was after joining this afterschool program, where I took classes with students from other high schools, that I realized that I wasn't so "smart." I was labeled the "smartest" student in my high school, but when I was competing with students from other schools, all of a sudden I did not know so much. I found myself wondering why my teachers did not teach me the things these students knew, or at least made me aware of what students in my grade level ought to know. Through this program, I began to hear students talking about the colleges they wanted to go to. I always knew I wanted to go to college, because that's what good students ought to do (that's what I was told). But at the beginning of my junior year, I had no idea what I needed to do to get into college, I had no idea what the SAT was, I could not even name ten colleges in the United States.

The critical intervention was an out-of-school program that surrounded Natasha with resources and targeted support that helped her to negotiate the pathway to college. In reflecting back on her experiences, she concluded:

After taking some courses at Smith in regards to how the American society is structured, a feeling of distress came over me. Feelings of guilt, betrayal, disappointment, anger, and many other feelings began to boil up inside me. I felt guilty that I was the one who "made it" and my friends and classmates didn't; I began to compare my own struggle with theirs, and I wondered why I made it to college and they didn't. I found myself wondering about whether they would have gone to college if they had my program.

Another student who attended an urban squash program in Boston described her program as family.

We played squash, but there was so much more. We went to tournaments at colleges and visited museums. We studied with our coaches, took SAT courses, and our squash instructors nagged us to get our work done. School was different. The program was family and school was a place I went and I never felt connected in the same way.

As we heard these stories, we found ourselves intrigued by the educational and policy implications of a movement that appeared to be serving high-need children through innovative practices that outwardly resisted the testing and accountability mania sweeping through schools. We were also drawn to such programs because we had participated in variations of them ourselves while growing up in Brooklyn, attending and teaching in public schools, and working within the community. When we met at Smith College about twelve years ago, our conversation unfolded around the myriad of overlapping experiences and interests of our childhood. We reminisced about how the reinforced rims and metal backboards on the basketball courts in Flatbush's Marine Park were unforgiving unless you shot with hefty backspin; we needled each other about the great rivalry between James Madison High School on Bedford Avenue, which was where Don played during the early 1960s, and nearby Sheepshead Bay High School, where Sam taught and coached in the late 1980s. The "'epic rivalry'" banter ended quickly when Don asked Sam if Sheepshead could match Madison's current roster of alums: three senators (Charles Schumer, D-NY; Norm Coleman, R-MN; and Berrnie Sanders, I-VT), and a Supreme Court justice (Ruth Bader Ginsberg).

Once the storytelling ended, our conversation turned toward our professional interests, and we discovered that we still clung to our Brooklyn roots in that the central questions of our professional work were derived from the experiences of growing up in the city. Don was concerned with questions about how people develop skill and expertise and the role that coaching and teaching play in the process of overall development. Sam's professional interests focused on how young people engaged or disengaged in school—particularly urban schools.

A significant crossroads in our work occurred in the spring of 2002 when Don received a call from the executive director of a large Boston-based private foundation. She conveyed that her foundation had been supporting various Boston Public Schools initiatives and, in particular, out-of-school programs. The preliminary research that they commissioned revealed that many children were dismissed as early as 1:30 in the afternoon, and that a fair percentage of those kids were involved in an array of afterschool programs. To no one's surprise, sports was one of the most popular activities. Knowing that Don had been a coach and an educator who had taught and researched various aspects of sports, she asked him what he thought about the idea of sports as a medium through which youth could acquire knowledge, skills, and attitudes that would help them in the classroom.

Don agreed to conduct a two-tiered study that began with a systematic review of the research literature followed by a study of Boston programs doing work in this domain. The survey included multiple site visits and interviews with program founders and executive directors. These encounters introduced him to an emerging and dynamic field populated by energized and entrepreneurial individuals embracing the idea that sports can serve as a core activity to teach an array of psychosocial skills, while also providing an incentive for engaging kids in other activities such as tutoring, community service, and building social capital through mentoring.

What he found most remarkable was that such programs were being conceived and started around the "kitchen table" or other informal settings where young people brainstormed about what they really wished to do with the rest of their lives. Most had attended competitive colleges, some had advanced or professional degrees, and many had already tested the waters in occupations they thought they wanted to pursue, but now found unfulfilling. Many had been exceptional athletes and conveyed to Don how rewarding those activities had been for them. In turn, they envisioned that sports, and the transformative experiences they provided, had the potential to strongly benefit kids who had little going for them. At this point these programs were in their infancy, as developers tried to figure out how their general ideas about sports as a medium for youth development could be operationalized. In other words, Don was seeing firsthand how cadres of entrepreneurs were striving to create programs that used lacrosse, squash, crew, tennis, and other outdoor activities to enhance and literally save the lives of young urban youth. His report concluded that sports, when done in a manner in which skill development, physical activity, and teamwork were prioritized over winning, children's health and well-being were positively impacted. However, it was still too soon to determine whether sport involvement could affect the academic achievement of participants.

In the meantime, Sam remained at Smith College, teaching and continuing to build a connection between Smith and urban schools in Holyoke and Springfield. The focus of the emerging partnership was on programs that ferried college students taking courses in education or related fields to the North End neighborhood of Springfield, where they provided tutoring and academic support for elementary and middle school students. Each semester nearly sixty-five students participated in the program.

A primary site for this program was the Gerena Elementary School. The principal, a short, dynamic, and irrepressible presence, had grown up in Springfield and his own children had attended Gerena. Faced with critically low student achievement, the principal was relentlessly trying to infuse Gerena with resources. His refrain whenever he spoke with Sam was, "We'll take whatever you can provide. Our students need so much." College students would arrive during the day to support teachers and students during class time—tutoring individual students or guiding small math or reading groups. The program was successful in getting college students involved in a sustained community effort, but the school continued to struggle.

In late 2002, Gerena was notified that its chronic low performance meant that the school had to submit to a "School Panel Review Process." The review entailed an investigation of the school by a panel to "assist the Commissioner of Education in determining whether State intervention is needed to guide improvement efforts in schools where students' MCAS performance is critically low and no trend toward improved student performance is evident from MCAS data."[1] As a community partner, Sam was asked to participate in a focus group during the review. During the session, he was asked to describe the scope and structure of the program. At the end of the session, one of the reviewers looked up from her notes and said matter-of-factly, "This sounds like an impressive effort. We heard from teachers and others that the benefit is that maybe some of the students have expanded their vocabulary from being around the college students." Her implication was clear. The program was noble, but the children of Gerena needed something more.

Fortuitously, just as the Gerena review was ending, Don returned from Boston with a proposal to imagine something more. After Don concluded his research, the foundation offered to fund an initiative that would attempt to operationalize what he had learned in his study of Boston-based youth sport programs. In other words, the gauntlet was thrown: "You have studied it; you have written coherently about it. But can you do it?"

TAKING A DEEPER LOOK: STUDYING WHAT'S OUT THERE AND WHAT'S POSSIBLE

Our first response, as academics, was to pursue further study. We immediately assembled an informal group of professors, undergraduates, and graduate students to expand on research already done. From our study group readings and discussions we learned a great deal about the various battles being fought over education in the political realm, what futuristic economists were forecasting with regard to the country's global competitiveness, and how a narrowing of the public school curriculum was obscuring the development of skills, problem-solving capacities, and dispositions toward work that were deemed critical for success in the twenty-first century. These included the ability "to think critically and solve problems, work in teams and lead by influence, be agile and adaptable, take initiative and be entrepreneurial, communicate clearly and concisely, access and analyze information effectively, and be curious and imaginative."[2]

A key reading in the development of our thinking was Richard Rothstein's *Class and Schools*.[3] He made the case that much of what has become known as the academic achievement gap was attributable to other sorts of gaps that existed among kids from different socioeconomic strata, such as health, housing, employment, and an array of what he labeled "non-cognitive skills."[4] Rothstein identified such things as communication capacity, interpersonal skills, motivation and initiative, work ethic, and adaptability to change. Along with other prominent theorists such as Robert Halpern and Reed Larson, he contended that these attributes, while critical for school success, may best be cultivated in out-of-school programs in which youth development is a primary focus.[5]

In conjunction with our study group, we embarked on a series of conversations with local educators and community members. We had no overarching conceptual method or approach to arranging these conversations other than to meet individuals working at the intersection of education, athletics, health, and community. In the course of these discussions, two key learnings emerged: first, no matter how grim the statistics were involving poverty, academic achievement, or health in a particular community or neighborhood, people were proud of their community and believed that positive changes were occurring. Second, community members were deeply suspicious of our academic affiliation. College and community partnership may mean one thing to academics, but among community members accustomed to researchers who arrive, extract their data, and vanish, there is rampant skepticism about the motives and commitment of representatives from the academy. After months of study and conversations, we decided to pilot a program.

LAUNCHING PROJECT COACH

Our breakthrough moment came during a conversation with a local principal who suggested that we speak to the neighborhood parks and recreation director, whom he described as a "legend in the community." We met him in an office covered with pictures of youth playing sports and he took us on a tour of the neighborhood complex, which included an elementary school, a middle school, a library, and a health center. When we walked over to the middle school, he said, "Let me show you our pride and joy." He took us out back and showed us three well-greened soccer fields.

> We are so proud of these fields. Five years ago these fields were abandoned and overgrown. They had all kinds of junk on them and car wrecks, and they were a favorite hangout for all sorts of dangerous characters, including drug dealers. This was no place parents

wanted their kids around, but we received a federal grant and transformed them.

We responded by saying, "You must be so thrilled to see your youth playing on those fields now." He paused and then replied, "Actually, these fields get used more often by the elite soccer teams from the suburbs. The kids from the neighborhood don't usually use them." Surprised, we asked, "Why not?" "I have interest from the kids," he said, "but I can't find coaches. I just can't find a core of parent volunteers to serve as coaches. If I could find enough coaches, I could use the fields." We asked, "Do you think you could find high school students who would want to get paid to be coaches?" "Absolutely," he responded. "I know so many kids who would love to."

Out of this conversation, the seed of Project Coach emerged. We began modestly, with virtually no budget and staff. We did it all: from teaching the lessons, to hauling the water out to the fields, to vacuuming the room after a meeting. It turns out this is a typical beginning for these kinds of programs. Every program founder we talked with—even those who now run programs with multimillion-dollar budgets—described how their programs began as fragile, fledgling, and hesitant endeavors. As one executive director of a program that is now housed in a multimillion-dollar facility said, "I don't know what I was thinking when I began. I started by taking kids from the school that I was working at down to the tennis courts. They had no idea about tennis and I was just doing it because it felt like the right thing to do."

The driving idea behind Project Coach involves mobilizing teens—most of whom fall into demographic categories encumbered with designations such as low-income, at-risk, and vulnerable—to do good and important work in their community. We leverage the natural charisma, energy, and playfulness of adolescents and capitalize on the intrinsic fascination younger children have with older youth by structuring a program that puts them in the iconic role of "coach" to elementary-aged children. From a very modest beginning in which we taught 8 to 10 adolescents to coach soccer and basketball for 25 to 30 younger children at a Boys and

Girls Club, the program has grown dramatically; we now work with 60 adolescents representing all five high schools in Springfield, Massachusetts, and over 250 younger children from three elementary schools on soccer, volleyball, basketball, and rowing. As well, each coach is tutored for two hours a week by a college student we call a "personal-academic coach," and, in turn, adolescents help their players complete their homework before coaching them in a sport. Adolescent coaches also read sports-themed children's books with their players as a team. Moreover, we now monitor our coaches' schoolwork, provide college advising, and take them to visit campuses in the Northeast. Recently, the program added a social worker to deal with unique issues that may divert adolescents from participating fully in the program. Project Coach now also provides dinner for coaches and their players and organizes community-sport events for players' families. (See appendix A for a fuller description of Project Coach.)

As with other programs that we visited, Project Coach's expansion in number and breadth of activities is a response to individual and community needs. As we have all learned, for kids to thrive, they need an array of activities and supports, and programs are increasingly recognizing that they need to be doing a great deal more than simply engaging kids in the thematic activities with which they started. Project Coach has coaching as its core, but to categorize it simply as a "sports program" greatly distorts what we think is really going on. We are much more interested in the day-to-day development of the kids than in their futures as coaches and athletes.

In addition, we didn't begin this endeavor with the idea of writing a book. Even after we launched Project Coach, we kept trying to learn more about how to make our program better. We visited other programs, spoke to other directors and practitioners, watched programs in action, read everything we could, scoured the web, attended conferences, and learned through failure, frustration, and the occasional triumph. We came to understand that we are part of an emerging movement that strives to support underserved children by creatively using the time that youth have outside of school. The programs vary widely in focus: dance, arts, sports, theater, poetry, media arts, radio, chess, and more. The driving logic behind the programs hinges on what is sometimes called the "9% challenge."[6] That number comes from the fact that, upon graduation from high school, the typical American student will have spent only 9 percent of his or her time in school. This low dosage of schooling in relation to other activities calls into question the hypothesis that schools alone should be or can be centrally responsible for educational achievement and the acquisition of crucial life skills. It also recognizes that social, political, and economic changes that can alter the life circumstances of youth involve seismic shifts that can't be counted on to happen from within the school system alone.

WRITING A BOOK

From our journey as researchers, practitioners, and colleagues, we increasingly felt compelled to share what we were learning with others whom we had met along the way, and with those aspiring to become part of this rapidly evolving world. Our book describes numerous out-of-school programs, with special emphasis on four core programs animated by the principles of positive youth development, though we occasionally weave in anecdotes and observations from nearly 30 other programs that we encountered in our travels. (See appendix B for descriptions of these programs and appendix C for a partial list of people interviewed for the book.)

After a decade of thinking about youth development, running Project Coach, and observing others doing similar work, we conclude that the best programs are communities able to foster powerful relationships by engaging kids in activities that they find intrinsically rewarding. By working and playing together, youth acquire an array of qualities that help them to think, feel, and behave productively as they acquire requisite knowledge and skills. In essence, over time youth become what they do in their programs. Not only do we see talented athletes, artists, musicians, and coaches developing from these programs, but these youth also graduate from high school and enroll in college at rates well beyond what would be expected for kids coming from their demographic group.

This book offers an analytic view of these programs from a variety of perspectives, including those of the youth participants, school-based adults such as teachers and administrators, researchers, parents, staff, founders, and the philanthropists and foundation officers who fund the programs, as well as our own sense of the work as practitioners. While the book researches out-of-school programs, at its core, it focuses on the general conditions and structures able to engage youth in meaningful work. We believe that these programs provide a provocative and innovative response to a question important to all who work with and for youth: How do you engage youth in meaningful and productive educational experiences? This is a question that should be of interest to all who care about the education and development of young people.

Our book is organized around the questions that guided our exploration of these programs. We began by trying to understand the role that out-of-school programs play in the lives of underserved children. We address this in chapter 1, which describes how programs strive to enhance the social, cultural, and educational development of children. While we describe programs focused on helping youth develop expertise in a specific activity such as art or sports, the true mission of these programs involves providing developmentally beneficial opportunities for youth.

Chapter 2 contends with what we came to understand as the essential structural dilemma of these programs. Simply put, if these programs are to have a positive impact on the youth they aspire to serve, then they must keep kids involved and committed over time (in many cases, years) in activities that are both intense and demanding, while also remaining voluntary. How do they do it? Chapter 3 explores how programs cultivate a shared passion and devise norms, values, and processes that enable young people of different ages to develop a distinct identity around an activity and then grow and learn together over time. We came to understand that the distinctive power of these organizations resides in their ability to forge communities of practice where youth feel heard, loved, challenged, and competent.

Chapters 4 through 7 address a question that intrigued us within minutes of visiting the first program: What practices guide these programs and how are they operationalized? These chapters are our effort to describe the common practices and principles that animate these programs. In them we define the essential process as the cultivation of what we call the supercognitives, by which we mean critical capacities foundational to success at any endeavor. The four supercognitives we examine are as follows: Chapter 4 examines how programs cultivate a mastery mindset in their participants. This mindset is an amalgamation of qualities central to learning such as self-control, emotional regulation, and grit. Chapter 5 focuses on the importance of youth finding intrinsic satisfaction through participation in the program. We highlight how programs achieve this by helping youth gain competence in core activities, develop satisfying relationships with fellow participants and staff, and acquire a sense of control and autonomy over their commitment to the program. Chapter 6 addresses how programs help youth expand their sphere of social capital. This includes meeting new people and developing connections beyond the circles of their neighborhood and community. Chapter 7 focuses on perhaps the most critical challenge facing all such programs: How can attitudes, skills, and values acquired in one setting, such as an out-of-school program, be transferred to another setting, such as school or community life? For example, if a young woman becomes an excellent dancer through hard work and perseverance, how can a program encourage her to deploy the same grit in her school and community life?

The final chapter of the book became a focus of much of our discussion with youth. As teachers and researchers who work in schools, we tried to understand what makes youth programs distinctive from school. We conclude by exploring some practices that schools might learn from these programs.

CHAPTER ONE

The Promise of
Out-of-School Programs

Four afternoons a week we drive past the storied Grécourt Gates that frame the manicured campus of Smith College, where we both work as full professors. We navigate through the bustle of tourists and visitors in the quaint New England downtown of Northampton, Massachusetts, and merge onto I-91 south for a picturesque eighteen-mile drive past the meandering Connecticut River to the east and sprawling Mt. Tom to the south. Exit 11S brings us to Birnie Avenue in the North End of Springfield, a city of 154,000 that ranks sixth in the country for the number of children in poverty.[1] Our destination is the scuffed and airless gym of the Gerena Community School.

Inside the gym, the activity level is high and almost frenetic. The acoustics of the space amplify noise, and there is a jarring cacophony of bouncing balls, skidding sneakers, shrieking voices, and the clanging of loose basketball rims. We watch as sixteen-year-old Tomas strides over to a bustling amoeba-shaped group of elementary-aged boys and girls. He puts his whistle to his mouth and gives one short but decisive tweet. "OK, gather around for the huddle." Twelve boys and girls scamper over and sprawl in a fidgety circle where they are joined by Tomas and another teenager. Both teens wear neat blue tennis shirts emblazoned with "Coach."

"Coach Andre and I are happy to see you today. Before we begin playing, I have a question for you." Coach Tomas looks down at an index card he is clutching. After checking the card, he asks, "What does being a good sport mean to you?" Coach Tomas and fifteen-year-old Coach Andre listen intently as each player shares an idea. They ask follow-up questions like, "How does it feel if your opponent celebrates too much after scoring a basket?"

Off to the side following the back-and-forth is a red-shirted graduate student mentor. Coach Greg—a former college basketball player from Haverford College—nods enthusiastically and gives a thumbs-up signal as Andre works at eliciting responses from each of his players. Once all the young players have offered a thought, Coach Andre, who is a towering six feet five, pounds his meaty hands together in a drumroll, points to a thirty-foot square demarcated by orange cones, and says, "OK—everybody grab a basketball. There is the ocean. You are fishies—Coach Tomas and I are sharks. You know the game—LET'S GO!" In an instant the elementary students are tearing around the court, chased by their teenage coaches.

Andre, Tomas, and Greg work in our afterschool program Project Coach. We operate in a neighborhood that is among the poorest in the state of Massachusetts and one beset by an array of challenges, including low graduation rates, high rates of gang activity, and punishing cycles of generational underemployment. Teenagers from this community often get labeled at-risk and are viewed as vulnerable or dangerous by society. Our program leverages the natural charisma and playfulness of adolescence by structuring opportunities for these teens to serve as coaches of young children from their neighborhood. (See appendix D, "Notes for New Staff Members.")

Any adult who has volunteered to serve as a youth sport coach appreciates the complexity of coaching children, supervising physical activity, and negotiating the many tensions that arise when events involve children, parents, and competition. It is this authentic complexity that provides our teens and staff with a near-endless flow of dilemmas, conflicts, and, ultimately, teachable moments.

For example, Tomas and Andre have now transitioned to a full-court basketball game. The level of play is wildly variable: some of the fourth graders have just mastered the rudiments of dribbling while others whiz around the court, showcasing their emerging ability to stutter-step and execute a crossover dribble fake. Two of the bigger boys cover each other; at one point an errant pass rolls to the middle of the court and both boys hustle after it and collide. They spring up, fists balled, heads bobbing, glaring at each other. Coach Tomas quickly moves his body in between the boys, blows the whistle, and signals for the group to keep playing.

Players race back and forth for a few minutes and then a long shot clanks off the front rim and ricochets toward the sideline. The two boys involved in the prior altercation scramble toward the ball. As they get close, their eyes pull away from the ball and they lower their shoulders and careen into each other. Before they hit the ground they are flailing away at each other. The coaches spring into action. Coach Tomas steps assertively between the two boys. Coach Andre puts a meaty hand on the shoulder of the boy on his team and walks him right off the floor and into the hallway. Two other teenagers who serve as assistant coaches mobilize, call a timeout, and take their respective teams beneath the baskets for a huddle.

Coach Andre kneels down next to his player. Even crouched down, he towers over him. "Let's take some breaths and just calm down. I know you're upset, but let's just breathe and calm down." Coach Andre models what he means as he takes exaggerated long inhales and exhales. In the hallway, Coach Tomas is listening intently as his jittery fourth grader explains what happened. Our coaches have trained for this. Sports can be rough, and the court can be a place where conflicts erupt and tempers unravel. The teenagers are executing a Project Coach protocol that they have learned and practiced called S.C.A.P., which stands for separate, calm, actively listen, and problem-solve. After a few minutes of leaning down to be at eye level with the players, listening to the story, asking questions, and rehearsing options for when the two boys see each other again, the coaches will bring both boys together to resolve their conflict and come up with a plan if tensions should rise again.

The basketball game resumes and the two boys cover other players for the rest of the session. At the end of the game, once all the elementary-aged players have been dismissed, Greg calls the teens together. The circle starts out as a blob of nearly thirty teen coaches and ten staff swirling about in chaotic cross-cutting conversation, but Greg pulls them into a tight shoulder-to-shoulder circle. "Clap once if you can hear me!" He claps once—a loud snapping clap. The coaches clap in unison. "Clap three times if you can feel me." Three crackling choral claps echo back as the group coheres and focuses its attention on Greg. "Circle up into your home groups, begin with a short shout-out about something positive that happened in school today, then have each coach share one 'excellent' moment of the session, and then have each coach offer a suggestion about how to improve our work today." The large circle breaks apart into ten pods. Each group consists of three teenagers, a college student, and a staff member. The conversations appear animated, light-hearted, and focused. The gym buzzes with a zany, erratic adolescent energy despite the fact that it is 6 p.m. after a day that began at 5:45 a.m. for many of the high school students.

The post-mortem session derives from both the arena of sports, where coaches routinely call a team together to dissect a game and analyze game tape, and the field of teaching, where best practices in teacher education use reflection to examine how and why events transpired the way they did. After five minutes or so, Greg calls the larger group back together and asks if anybody wants to share a lesson learned that they will carry back to their own life in school or at home. Several coaches raise their hands, but Greg calls on Coach Andre. "We had a fight today during the game and I talked about two things in my small group that I want to share," he says. "First, we kind of messed up because before the fight happened there was an incident, and we just went on playing and didn't deal with it. If we dealt with it when it was just a little thing, we could have stopped it from becoming a big thing. And yeah . . . " His voice trails off. At this point, one of the staff members who had been debriefing with Coach Andre prompts him: "What did we talk about in relation to how that connects to our lives?" Coach Andre breaks into a toothy grin and says, "Oh yeah, we talked about so many times the conflicts we get into never start all of a sudden, but they build up. We talked about how important it is to deal with stuff and try and work it through, or help friends work it through before it blows up." Greg smiles, claps his hands together, and asks, "Anybody else?" Before somebody else can talk, Coach Andre steps into the middle with his hands held up as if he is stopping a car at an intersection. "Wait, wait, one more thing. I also did the breathing with my kids and it worked." He pantomimes bowing with deep, Zen-like breathing. The group cracks up.

The thirty-five or so laughing teenagers in the circle are growing up in a complicated and fraught environment. As teenagers they are on a high-stakes journey of development. Every day, all day—in school, with their friends, in their community—they are experimenting, testing, exploring, and trying on different roles, identities, and behaviors. Negotiating adolescence is chock-full of both significant episodes and everyday dilemmas that can hold significant consequences for the expanse of one's life.

They are a motivated group—like most of America's teenagers. Their ambitions match the national norm for American teenagers, over 90 percent of whom aspire to graduate from college. Take Coach Andre, whose work on the playing fields and in the gyms demonstrates a range of impressive high-level capacities. He is a good decision maker, an excellent communicator, a savvy reader of social cues, and a committed community activist. Coach Andre would seem to have the world in front of him, and maybe he does, but here is another glimpse of Coach Andre.

> Sam was driving and Don was in the passenger seat. Seven teens from our out-of-school program were in the back. We always tried to use the commute time to talk about meaningful subjects, and on this day we were asking about career aspirations. Andre, a boisterous fifteen-year-old Latino freshman from Springfield, was in the far back and he eagerly broadcast his aspirations. "I want to be one of those doctors. You know, the kind that does operations on the brain." Don responded, "You mean a neurosurgeon?"
>
> Andre said, "Yeah, I had an aunt who had to have that kind of surgery. I want to do that. They make mad money and help people."
>
> Sam then asked, "Do you know the process for becoming a doctor?" Andre responded, "Don't you have to go to college?" Don answered, "That is just the beginning. You have four years of college,

four years of medical school, and then some number of years after graduating from medical school where you apprentice. Sometimes it can be more than five years of being an intern."

The van got quiet. After an instant, Andre chimed back, "OK. I guess I'll do collision bodywork with my uncle. It's like the same thing."

In a different context, our repartee with Andre might be funny, but we're two middle-class college professors and researchers whose own children have done well in middle-class schools, and who have spent many years in our career teaching about the structural inequalities of the American educational system. We're in the van because the central mission upon which Project Coach is founded is to help youth like Andre navigate their teenage years and the pathway to college. Andre's statement is not funny; it's heartbreakingly sad because his life forecast is corroborated by an overwhelming corpus of empirical data.

Andre lives in a city that has the sixth-highest child poverty rate in the country. He attends a high school that graduates only about 45 percent of its students. He lives with his mother, who speaks only Spanish at home. He is poor. Despite his circumstances, his initial aspirations resonate with our highest ideals of the American dream: all children, regardless of their socioeconomic circumstances or race, can become successful if they work hard and acquire a first-rate education in our nation's schools.

This ideology anchors our individual and collective consciousness and is based on the belief that one's life outcome hinges on personal effort and talent. Education has historically been considered a force for equality in American society, capable of lifting less advantaged children and improving their life chances. Public schooling—as a core institution—was seen as the mechanism by which individuals could cultivate their potential. You don't have to look far into our past to find evidence that supports how this credo effectively functioned as the guiding principle of mobility and success in American life. As Duncan and Murnane note in their volume *Whither Opportunity: Rising Inequality, Schools, and Children's Life Chances,* between 1947 and 1977, a period in which the gross domestic product

(GDP) per capita doubled, the incomes of the poorest families nearly doubled as well. They write: "In fact, for the first three-quarters of the twentieth century, economic growth was a rising tide that lifted the boats of the rich and poor alike."[2] Crucial to this economic growth and the consequent boost to living standards was a rapid increase in educational attainment. In 1900, only 6 percent of teenagers graduated from high school, and only 3 percent of young people graduated from college. The comparable figures in 1975 were 75 and 23 percent, respectively.

By many indicators, this progress has stalled. Our country's vision of itself as a meritocratic system that rewards hard work and talent has been fundamentally called into question. Recent research on the achievement gap reveals that despite significant public policy efforts, the gap between rich and poor children is widening, a development that threatens to dilute education's leveling effects. Reardon analyzed a range of test and income data and reports, "The achievement gap between children from high- and low- income families is roughly 30 to 40 percent larger among children born in 2001 than among those born twenty-five years earlier. In fact, it appears that the income achievement gap has been growing for at least fifty years."[3] Sadly, in contrast to our belief that upward mobility comes from hard work, taking initiative, and getting a good education, recent data shows that educational mobility, which is defined as a young person's education relative to that of his parents, is slowing down.[4]

Policy makers, politicians, activists, and others have long vowed to close this achievement gap because the benefits for successfully graduating from college have never been higher. However, the resources available to low-income families to pay for their children's preschool, for access to good public schools or to private education, and for college investments have fallen farther behind those of affluent families.[5] In the face of these realities, there is no shortage of ideas and proposals. Two distinctive approaches to redressing the achievement gap have typically dominated the discourse and policy efforts. The first contends that by improving schools we can close the gap. The second asserts that school-based reform is not systemic enough to counteract the influence of social class characteristics, no matter the quality of the school.

School-based reformers believe that we should expect schools to close the achievement gap. They argue that if schools serving low-income children were run more effectively, they could close this gap and offset the array of social and economic factors alleged to be responsible for educational inequities. The school as engine of change focuses relentlessly on achieving academic outcomes that are measured through standardized test scores.[6]

In contrast, ecological and community reformers argue that schools alone cannot solve the problems of chronic poverty. These analyses of the achievement gap contend that children who grow up in poor families and in segregated, vulnerable communities with high rates of violence, joblessness, and isolation begin school with dramatically different and unequal circumstances, and thus we should expect them to perform in and leave school with unequal skills and abilities.[7] This view does not discount the importance of school quality in closing the achievement gap, but holds that other critical factors also must be addressed if we are to expect equality of educational outcomes across unequal demographic groups.

OUT-OF-SCHOOL PROGRAMS: ENGAGING, EXCITING, EMPOWERING

Ten years ago, we probably fell into the camp that believed schools were the fulcrum that could lift the academic achievement of young people. We recognized the pernicious barriers and impediments that poverty poses in healthy child development, but we believed in the promise of teaching and schools as a transformative lever in the lives of young people.

Our understanding of these issues has evolved through our work in Project Coach. The venture has been deeply rewarding and incredibly complicated. It is the most important work of our professional careers. It has changed our lives.

In the course of writing this book, we visited programs across the country that billed themselves as focused on sports, music, art, radio, and writing. Some were housed in multimillion-dollar facilities and others borrowed space from local schools or were tucked into shabby neighborhood storefronts. Each had a distinctive emphasis, but the thread running through these programs was their ability to build an ethos and community that engaged young people. What knitted these programs together was the quality of excitement and energy that youth demonstrated and described.

In an article that has been important to the youth development movement, the psychologist Reed Larson hones in on an observation that speaks forcefully to anybody who has ever taught, coached, or parented a teen. He contends that the central question in youth development is "how to get adolescents' fires lit, how to have them develop the complex of dispositions and skills needed to take charge of their lives."[8]

In other words, the project of youth development begins by sparking interest and then engaging young people cognitively, behaviorally, and emotionally so that they put forth the concentrated and purposeful effort necessary for achievement. That, more than anything, was the thread running through the many programs we examined. But we were looking to learn something more. Larson's dictum challenges us to view youth work as beginning with a spark, but to aspire to something extraordinarily more challenging. It is difficult enough to develop a program that secures the fickle attention of youth, but it is even more complicated to devise one that sustains their focus and commitment over time when competing against a myriad of alluring alternatives. The improbable mission of these programs is to provide the wraparound support that a vulnerable young person needs to graduate from high school, go to college, flourish in their personal development, and aspire toward a positive future. In other words, we set out to study programs that "lit the fire" but also did something more.

We didn't begin this project as a research endeavor, but as practitioners absorbed in the work and desperate to learn from others. Our method was simple: we asked everybody we met, "What programs do you know that are doing good work? Who do you know that is doing interesting work on out-of-school time?" We learned buckets from watching, listening, and then returning to Project Coach and attempting to implement what we learned with modifications that made sense for our program and our local context. Importantly, the programs we mention here are those we had direct contact with over the years. We also have had casual exposure to many other wonderful programs and staff that are equally deserving of coverage.

In deciding which programs to profile in this book, we developed a set of criteria that emerged from the many interviews that we did with present and past participants, and with program directors and staff.

First, the programs must have adequate breadth, intensity, and duration to impact a child's life. Typically, such programs include a complex mixture of academic, technical, multicultural, social, and emotional skills learning, in which contact occurs multiple times each week for many weeks.[9] This criterion also dovetails with conclusions reached by Bohnert, Fredricks, and Randall, who state that "research using both variable- and person-centered analytic strategies across a range of samples and ages suggests that getting involved in various activity contexts (i.e., breadth) is beneficial to youth development, particularly relating to academic outcomes."[10] They go on to report that intensity and duration of involvement have been positively related to an array of academic and psychological outcomes.

Second, it is becoming widely accepted that the length of adolescence is extending to the mid to late twenties—a period sometimes called emerging adulthood—and the pathways to becoming independent adults have become more ambiguous and numerous. Consequently, we selected programs that reflect such complexity and work with youth across a wide age range, from elementary school to, and increasingly through, college.

Third, we sought out programs that focus on positive development rather than prevention of dysfunctional behavior associated with, for example, substance abuse, violence, and teen pregnancy. The selected programs hinge on the idea that one needs skills, knowledge, and a variety of other personal and social assets to function well during adolescence and adulthood. Typically, this encompasses physical health, cognitive and social development, and psychological and emotional well-being. This approach has roots in the emerging field of positive psychology and contends that the path to vitality entails youth becoming motivated, directed, socially competent, compassionate, and psychologically vigorous.[11] These qualities—which the research literature identifies as critical predictors of academic achievement and psychological health—are rarely taught explicitly or emphasized systematically in schools too often obsessed with narrow cognitive outcomes.[12]

A fourth criterion was that they articulate a macro-view of their role as an out-of-school program that addresses the academic achievement gap. This is consistent with Weis and Dimitriadis, who argue that to view out-of-school time as unconnected from that in school may be a disservice to youth who are growing up in an intensely competitive "New Economy World." We can no longer valorize youth practices as disconnected from their broader context because the linkage between "success" in school (defined in particular ways, such as test scores and academic attainment) and economic and social mobility is becoming tighter than ever.[13]

Fifth, while selected programs focus on improving school performance, they are not school programs. In fact, they intentionally cultivate an identity as a nonschool organization and often view school and its constraining policies as detrimental to healthy development—and for good reason. In all sorts of research studies, youth describe school as uniformly boring and disengaging.[14] The epidemic of disengagement is particularly devastating to poor and low-income youth. As a National Research Council report on increasing school engagement concluded, "When students from advantaged backgrounds become disengaged, they may learn less than they could, but they usually get by or they get second chances; most eventually graduate and move on to other opportunities. In contrast, when students from disadvantaged backgrounds in high-poverty, urban high schools become disengaged, they are less likely to graduate and consequently face severely limited opportunities."[15] The programs we describe in this book seek to provide a counternarrative to the institutional dreariness of school by organizing programming around activities that youth find engaging, exciting, and empowering.[16]

While we visited many outstanding programs, we decided to focus on three programs, in addition to Project Coach, that met the five criteria and were located in the Northeast. Their proximity enabled us to conveniently visit and to meet many of the kids who were products of these programs. Following is a snapshot of each program.

Project Coach: Based in Springfield, Massachusetts, this program puts teens in the role of sport coach. The curriculum focuses on developing key leadership attributes such as strategic thinking, problem solving, communications, emotional control, and conflict resolution. Coaches work with Smith College faculty and students on a range of projects associated with health and community wellness, from coaching elementary youth and running sport leagues to researching obesity rates at local schools and providing parent education on community health issues. The program uses an expanded definition of the role of coach to provide teens with a range of experiences designed to build their ability to plan and execute challenging tasks.

StreetSquash: This New York City–based program uses squash as a "hook" to engage underserved kids to become part of a community that can support them athletically, academically, and socially. Sports, academic enrichment, community service, mentoring, and travel are blended together, with the ultimate goal of helping kids to do well academically, graduate from high school, and then graduate from college. StreetSquash is part of the National Urban Squash and Education Association, which now has twelve member programs in eleven cities that use this youth development model.

G-Row: A Boston-based rowing program for adolescent girls, G-Row combines sports, academic enrichment, mentoring, and health education. As with many sports programs, it aims to teach an array of general attributes such as self-confidence, determination, and the tenacity to overcome hardships associated with a physically and psychologically demanding activity. Research throughout the years has shown that urban girls participate in sports less than any other youth group, and drop out at higher rates.[17] Consequently, the chance to learn more about a successful program focused on female adolescent development through a "nontraditional" sport such as rowing, which has somewhat of an elitist reputation, was captivating.

Artists for Humanity: This Boston-based program uses art as a core activity to teach underserved youth self-sufficiency and social justice through paid employment in the arts. Studios include painting, photography, sculpture, screen printing, and web media. Through training and apprenticeships, youth hone their artistic skills, and as working artists, they develop the professional and intrapersonal/interpersonal skills necessary to fulfill commissions in the world of commercial art. Participants are expected to maintain satisfactory academic records and, when necessary, engage in tutoring to meet the academic requirements of the program.

Interestingly, three of the four programs we identified as models are associated with sports. In our research on out-of-school programs, we consistently discovered that sports programs were more intent on building a bridge between their work and school. We hypothesize that the general advancement of sports programs in this regard is related to the ongoing pressure that such programs face in proving their worth to funders. Sports programs can be construed as "ornamental" to academic development or focused on what sports writer Jimmy Cannon once called "the toy department of life." This conception of sports hurts programs in a competitive marketplace where achieving measurable academic and developmental results is the metric used to allocate grant funds and determine worth. For sports programs to be noticed and sustain their sources of funding, they have to be innovative and entrepreneurial in developing systems that result not only in productive engagement in a sport, but also achievement in other domains.

FOUNDERS' PASSION: ENGAGING IN ACTIVITIES
CAN BE TRANSFORMATIVE

As we traveled, observed programs, and interviewed leaders of out-of-school organizations, it quickly became apparent to us that the founders and core leaders of this movement possessed a bold entrepreneurial energy. They viewed the achievement "gap problem," in metaphorical terms, as two trains leaving the same station at different times, with the one departing later trying to catch up to the one that left earlier. (Geoffrey Canada, the founder of the Harlem Children's Zone, has used this metaphor.) Their programs have attempted to provide a metaphoric turbocharged engine and fuel to enable the "delayed" train to catch up.

These activists preferred rolling up their sleeves and trying to actually do something to close the gap rather than simply theorizing, discussing, and acting only after all conceivable obstacles have been removed. We wanted to find out who these people were who start, nurture, and commit their lives to building the sorts of organizations that really make a difference in kids' lives.

Though each leader had a unique history, there seemed to be common threads that allowed us to build what might be construed as a composite prototype of the successful out-of-school organization founder/entrepreneur. In crafting this prototype we will allude to only a small sample of individuals, but from our many interactions with those who have created and/or led such programs, we think that the central themes identified accurately reflect who these people are and how they think about this work.

The first thing that struck us about these men and women was that they all had missionary zeal, were passionate about what they were doing or had done, and possessed a deep-seated belief that the focal activity of their program could be as transformative for others as it had been for them. Susan Rodgerson, who started Artists for Humanity as an artist-entrepreneur, stated, "I wanted to use my love of working with youth to empower them through the same process that had empowered me." She was a successful professional artist and social activist who had studied at the Art Institute of Boston and Radcliffe College, and exhibited widely. She understood how the process of producing art, as well as the resulting product, could both empower producers as individuals and promote their economic advancement.

Holly Metcalf, founder of G-Row, has talked about using rowing as her metaphor for the unity of people's mental and physical power, and how getting underserved youth involved in rowing can break down the sport's sexist, elitist, and racist reputation. She was a six-time national and Olympic champion, winning a gold medal in the 1984 Olympics and also an array of medals at the world championships between 1981 and 1987. She also lectured for Reebok to thousands of students about the power of sports to develop both mental and physical capacities. Holly attended Mt. Holyoke College and earned a master's degree from Harvard's Graduate School of Education, where she focused on risk prevention, human development, and psychology.

George Polsky, founder of StreetSquash, was totally focused on using squash as a medium and "hook" to help poor kids get to and graduate from college: "Whether or not a student can hit a great forehand isn't important. Whether or not a kid ends up being a great squash player doesn't really matter. What matters is getting a great education." He had been a co-captain of the Harvard squash team, which had won three national intercollegiate titles. He had also been all-Ivy and all-American, and subsequently played for the 1997 U.S. Maccabiah team, where he talked with a friend, Greg Zaff (a Williams College alum who later founded Squash-Busters), about using the sport as a medium to enhance the lives of disadvantaged youth. After college Polsky taught Spanish for four years in middle and high school, and then went on to get a degree in social work from NYU. Given his athletic, teaching, and social work background, it was natural that he also saw the confluence of these activities in the development of an urban squash program. As he has conveyed many times, his goal was to help kids graduate from high school and be accepted into college, not just teach them how to hit forehands.

We found similar patterns among the founders of other programs we visited. Greg Zaff echoed an equally compelling sentiment in stating that "persistence, discipline, and sportsmanship can be more than just a recipe for squash success; they can be a vehicle for remarkable change in kids' lives." He told us that while SquashBusters in Boston follows basic structures and processes in its day-to-day activities, it also does whatever is necessary to help any of its kids overcome obstacles to realizing their dreams.

Zack Lehman was very conscious of his privileged background, and besides viewing lacrosse as a means to teaching such life skills as responsibility, respect, effort, communication, and teamwork, he wanted to share an activity with inner-city youth that, for the most part, was available only to kids living in suburbia. For his first three years coaching for Charlestown Lacrosse, the precursor to MetroLacrosse, he did not take a penny in salary.

Julie Kennedy was willing to work ninety hours a week as a Teach for America teacher by day and a Starbucks barista by night, while running DC Scores in Washington in the afternoons. Julie was stunned to learn that the kids she taught had nowhere to go after school, and was convinced that there were holes in the school curriculum. Her soccer experiences as a girl growing up in Canada had convinced Julie that her students' out-of-school time could be used productively to teach such things as critical thinking, teamwork, communications, and self-confidence.

Bob Grove and Madeleine Steczynski were troubled by the wave of youth violence sweeping through Boston during the summer of 1991, and believed that if kids could become passionate about something like music, they could develop an array of capacities such as resilience, community mindedness, and the self-direction to be more productive. Their passion for the work was evident when they quit their paying day jobs to pursue their belief that music was a medium through which kids could find their voice, build personal assets, and become positive contributors to their communities. They created Zumix to help youth develop such assets and values.

As an aggregate, these founders seemed to begin with a general belief that getting kids involved in the activities that they themselves valued would produce positive outcomes. They did not seem to have clearly defined notions about causality or how specific activities would ameliorate the delayed starting points from which kids began, but they had a sense that what they were doing, or planned to do, would have a net benefit to closing the gap. One of the things that made this group unique was their penchant for action, and willingness to learn and figure things out along the way. Their temperaments and risk-taking mentalities very much reflected Schoenfeld's approach:

> Sometimes you have to build something to see if it will work . . . and then you have to study the hell out of it . . . this kind of approach does not represent a weak alternative to conducting controlled experiments but a different option altogether.[18]

In essence, these people deeply believed that their personal experiences with an activity that they loved could be configured in some way and shared with youth to produce the same life-changing benefits that they themselves had received. Though not calling it such, they were ascribing to the power of teaching kids to be focused, deliberate, conscientious, and able to self-regulate.

TAKING ON THE ROLE OF CONCERTED CULTIVATORS

While the programs they created centered on different activities, for the most part, these founders were remarkably similar in embracing an approach that went beyond the strict structures of the activities to redress the educational inequities derived from the social, economic, and political forces that largely marginalize the underserved. In essence, all were developing programs that operated with a logic that resembled what Annette Lareau in her classic study of child rearing labeled as "concerted cultivation."[19]

Lareau coined the term to describe the parenting practices she and her team observed to be typical of middle- and upper-income families. These parents see it as their duty to actively foster the development of their children's potential skills and talents. They act as their children's advocate and agent in an effort to make certain that they get exposed to an array of experiences, preparing them to better negotiate the maze of institutions, obstacles, and opportunities that lie between childhood and early adulthood. These include but extend beyond such things as using language with agility and nuance, thinking abstractly, reasoning and solving problems through negotiation rather than force, interacting effectively with adults, being a team player, managing time, advocating for oneself, learning to compete and to cooperate, solving the formula for succeeding in school, learning how to make organizational rules work in one's favor, and advocating for oneself.

Parents also help their children juggle a range of extracurricular activities and support their involvement by serving as coaches, transporters, funders, and advisors. With such assistance, these children have a higher probability of success in whatever they do than those youth whom Lareau observed growing up in a more "natural growth" framework. These are the children of working-class and poor families in which parents do not have the time, capacity, or financial resources to support their kids' out-of-school or in-school activities to the same degree as parents who are "concerted cultivators."

These gaps have always existed, but there is evidence to suggest that the disparities are increasing dramatically as income gaps separating rich and poor families widen. For example, one study found that in 1972, Americans at the upper end of the income spectrum were spending five times as much per child as low-income families. By 2007 that gap had grown to nine to one; spending by upper-income families more than doubled, while spending by low-income families grew by 20 percent. This means that

> wealthy parents invest more time and money than ever before in their children (in weekend sports, ballet, music lessons, math tutors, and in overall involvement in their children's schools), while lower-income families, which are now more likely than ever to be headed by a single parent, are increasingly stretched for time and resources. This has been particularly true as more parents try to position their children for college, which has become ever more essential for success in today's economy.[20]

In other words, some families have access to and can invest in soccer, piano, art, tutoring, or other enrichment programs, while others cannot. These investments are analogous to selecting children based on their parent's ability and willingness to pay for tracking them onto paths that cultivate an array of talents. When started early, and pursued over an extended time period, the cumulative effect becomes so large that less advantaged youth have virtually no way of catching up. These differences are what Lareau calls the "transmission of differential advantage to children."[21]

As we have observed from others and in our own program, over time, programs have become more intentional about serving as "concerted cultivators." Perhaps the most obvious examples of this are how the programs organize national and international travel opportunities, arrange for school placements and transfers, find scholarships to summer camps, organize college visits, connect with SAT preparation courses, and pair kids with adult mentors to engage in thematic and nonthematic program activities. In essence, a highly supportive environment is built around core program activities to fill gaps that might prevent kids from being competitive with peers from more privileged circumstances. These activities provide a type of "social bridging" in which less-privileged youth are provided opportunities to acquire the knowledge, skills, and values needed if they are to succeed in college and work in a world that may be quite different from the one they grew up in. Yet, as pointed out by many, these young people also need to remain connected to their families and communities. All of the programs we visited attempted to strengthen such bonds by organizing and requiring ongoing community service activities.

The programs that we explored reflected the interests, experiences, and personalities of their founders, who saw that, in one way or another, the path they traveled to their own accomplishments could be traversed by others. As a cohort, they have produced some remarkable organizations for underserved youth that are reducing the differential advantages enjoyed by more well-off children. Specifically, these programs embrace youth and expose them to a wide range of experiences and supportive people who make them feel like a valued part of a noble enterprise. By teaching a core activity, they engage youth cognitively, emotionally, and physically. In the process, they promote social interaction across age groups and generations, while bridging social and economic classes.

Most important, they help kids develop what we call supercognitives, which have often been called "noncognitives" or "soft skills."[22] These include, but are not limited to, such things as emotional regulation, attentional control, resilience in the face of setbacks or destructive social pressures, problem recognition and resolution, the capacity to avoid or manage conflict, the discipline to set goals and execute plans to fulfill them, and the ability to communicate effectively. To us, calling these important skills "noncognitive" or "soft" feels diminishing and, in many ways, dismissive. For example, can communication take place without cognition? Communication is an incredibly complex activity that is affective, cognitive, and physical. Our contention is that characterizing this array of skills as noncognitive or soft is a flawed premise that marginalizes important capacities as "ornamental" to a young person's development.

In an effort to recognize the complexity of these qualities, we use the term *supercognitives* in that they are more than merely cognitive; they employ multiple forms of intelligence and judgment in active service of behavior. They also have a generic quality that transcends contexts, and they are critical for success in any significant endeavor. Whether one is involved in sports, the arts, academics, or a profession, supercognitives are critical for developing the specific technical skills required within a domain. They are implicitly and explicitly learned—or not learned—from the formal and informal experiences youth have with their families, peers, communities, and schools. The challenge for those interested in educating youth, and specifically underserved students, is to develop and implement strategies for teaching them. Interestingly, it appears that many of the activities that are being cut in schools can be found in afterschool and summer programs, and may be the most appropriate settings for the teaching and learning of supercognitives. In the chapters that follow we share what we have learned about why these critical qualities are so important, and how a cluster of out-of-school programs are helping youth to acquire them. In chapter 2 we examine what research tells us about developing expertise in any endeavor, and how the programs that we observed utilize such information to help youth develop knowledge, skills, and values that promote success across contexts.

CHAPTER TWO

The Framework for Getting Good at Anything

It's a Volvo afternoon at Roberto Clemente Park. The parking lot, which backs up to an abandoned railroad track overgrown with hardy urban greenery like Japanese knotweed and sumac, is half full with late-model SUVs and sensible family cars, all sporting a splashy bright red Valley United Soccer Club (VUSC) decal on the back. A cluster of adults rim the sidelines, attuned to what is transpiring on the field. Dressed in khakis or fitted black yoga pants, they clutch their white and pastel Dunkin' Donuts or green Starbucks cups. They glance over at the Project Coach teenagers with a smidge of anxiety. It's the look that adults often get in the presence of teenagers they don't know—particularly teenagers of color.

Our young coaches drag bags of balls, stacks of cones, and portable goals to set up the soccer fields before our elementary-aged players show up from school. On the field, a VUSC coach with a British accent and wraparound sunglasses briskly cajoles his players to sharpen up their movement. "There you go, mate. Quicker now. Play quick."

Dropping our bags on the side, we watch. We often encouraged our coaches to watch other teams and coaches as part of their training. The VUSC coach is effortlessly in charge and his players buzz through cones, playing give-and-go with speed and skill.

Sebastian—one our most veteran coaches at age sixteen—lives almost directly across the street from the park. "I can't believe it," he says. "These kids play better than our varsity team."

The kids Sebastian is watching are nine and ten years old. They belong to the VUSC, a regional soccer club "dedicated to excellence in premier youth soccer." Sebastian asks, "Where do these kids come from? Do you know how good they'll be when they are our age?"

Our coaches look uncomfortable as they move onto the adjoining field. You can tell that they are self-conscious about their own skill compared to what they observe on the field. A normal set-up by our coaches is pretty raucous—lots of good-natured goofing around and blasting of balls. Today they are sedate as they prep the practice field. Soon our elementary players show up, looking ridiculously ragtag in comparison to the mini-professionals pinging the ball around the field. Aside from the quantum gap in skill and athleticism, other differences starkly stand out. All of the VUSC players zipping around the field are white. The schools encircling the fields are 98 percent Hispanic and black. All the youth in Project Coach are nonwhite.

As the two groups play side-by-side, other differences leap out. The VUSC players are all geared up: they have dry-fit athletic tee shirts and matching shorts and all of them wear cleats. None of our players wear cleats. Most wear long pants, and there are girls scampering around wearing skirts. The skill level of our players feels like a light-year behind the VUSC players'. Sebastian turns to me and says with a nervous grin, "It's like *Beauty and the Beast*." He looks at me, shakes his head, and in a voice tinged with puzzlement, sadness, and the threads of resentment, asks, "How did they get so good?"

It didn't register at the time, but Sebastian's question is one for the ages. He is asking—among other things—what explains the difference in performance between the kids he coaches and these other children? Why do they dramatically surpass in skill and knowledge the children he works with?

The inequities on display at Roberto Clemente Field are an allegory for what is transpiring across our country. The "achievement gap" that

Sebastian and his fellow coaches react to is not the typical test score gap we hear so much about. As wrenching as it can be to study the profound differences between the academic achievements of one group versus another, the comparisons are somewhat sanitized because they are represented as aggregated numbers on tests. What Sebastian and the other coaches react to on that field is an "in-your-face" gap that begets the question, How did this group get so good?

THE CONTEXT OF GAPS AND THE NATURE OF EXPERTISE

Over the past few decades an intriguing body of knowledge has evolved that provides a substantive answer to Sebastian's question—how do such significant disparities in achievement and performance occur? Researchers have endeavored to determine whether persons who have success in domains such as sports, the arts, academia, intellectual activities such as chess, and prodigious memory tasks are simply born for greatness or achieve it through other factors. Essentially, the literature corroborates Thomas Edison's oft-quoted observation: "Genius is 1 percent inspiration and 99 percent perspiration." Seemingly, he recognized the importance of hard work in producing great things, and minimized the significance of innate capacities.

Perhaps the most prominent researcher/writer who has studied the acquisition of expertise is Anders Ericsson.[1] His work seeks to explain the processes and mechanisms that lead to superior achievement across professions, from medical doctors to athletes to scientists.[2] The gist of this literature is that great achievements are typically the product of engaging in an activity for an extended time under the tutelage of a teacher or coach who can guide a student along a trajectory that leads from novice to expert status. "Ten years and ten thousand hours of practice" has been widely popularized as the minimum for reaching world-class performance across numerous endeavors—the key point being that expertise requires a great deal of effort expended over a very long time. To some extent, this dovetails with the extended day, week, and year schedules now common among charter schools such as the Knowledge Is

Power Program (KIPP), which emphasizes extended academic learning. KIPP's day runs from 7:30 a.m. to 5 p.m., with Saturday school twice a month and at least three weeks of mandatory summer school.[3] It also corresponds with the trend in youth sports and other activities that emphasize early training and systematic preparation.

One answer to Sebastian's question can be seen in a sign we saw posted at a local indoor soccer facility that many of the VUSC soccer players frequent during the winter. An advertisement for a toddler and youth soccer program, it states: "Soccer for Kids—Ages 18 months–9 Yrs" with a number for parents to call. In short, the children with whom we work are competing against kids who begin intensive preparation at an early age, accumulate many more hours of activity, receive focused and effective coaching, and become members of a group or community emphatically attentive to helping them get better. This formula for success profoundly shapes the difference in abilities that Sebastian observed.

Another element in gaining expertise entails how that time is spent: mere time on task is not enough. The time spent must be productive and structured to continuously cultivate greater skill. This typically means working on the edge of one's "envelope" and engaging in activities that are perceived as "hard," rather than simply repeating over and over again what one already knows and is able to do. For athletes this would mean developing new and more complex skills, higher levels of physical conditioning, and more sophisticated tactical knowledge. For a musician it would mean tackling more complex musical scores. Again, this is an objective of a large number of in-school and out-of-school programs targeting underserved populations. Nonetheless, the literature also recognizes that engaging in activities that "push the envelope" is not easy, and that the quality of engagement during this time is even more critical. For the most part, it is recognized that optimal practice and learning occurs in small increments of an hour or two distributed across a day, rather than as one continuous stream. As with virtually any activity, fatigue and disengagement are inversely related to duration of effort. Typically, athletes and musicians cannot practice productively for more than an hour or two at a time, nor can students focus on complex materials without breaks.

A third factor associated with acquiring expertise is the systematic input of a knowledgeable coach or teacher. Typically, this is a person, a group of people, or a series of persons and groups who provide inspiration, guidance, and systematic feedback regarding his or her development. Such a person or group serves in a supportive capacity and plots a trajectory that will get the individual from where they are to where they want to be. For a runner or swimmer in middle school who wishes to be an Olympian, this would entail assessing her current time, estimating what a competitive world-class time will be in four or eight years, and then plotting a course for decreasing her time incrementally by using short-term goals. Critical to such a program would be the coach's ability to teach the athlete stroke techniques, design conditioning sessions to develop aerobic and anaerobic capacities, and undertake a mental training program to help her deal with the stresses of training and competing.

Of critical importance in such a comprehensive program is the coach's ability to diagnose problems, provide meaningful prescriptive feedback, and push the athlete to go beyond her comfort level.[4] Ericsson coined the term "deliberate practice" to differentiate this more intentional approach to developing knowledge and skill from engagement and practice that is more haphazard and recreational. As some have observed, recreational athletes can play at an activity for many years and hit a performance plateau on which they seem to be fixed. In contrast to the "deliberately practicing" athlete who challenges himself to continuously learn new skills and perfect those already acquired, the recreational athlete simply repeats what he can do well, but rarely ventures into the risky terrain of what he cannot do, or does awkwardly. The systematic and focused activities of the VUSC team embody deliberate practice in that players work on explicit skills with a highly trained coach who offers ongoing technical and tactical feedback; the Project Coach approach involves general recreational play. Each has its advantages.

As an example, the following pages describe two programs that use the same afterschool time slot but in very different ways. The first description is from a private soccer program (see "Northampton Soccer Club: Program Description").

Northampton Soccer Club: Program Description

The Northampton Soccer Club Developmental Program will teach little ballplayers the fundamental individual skills of soccer through small-sided intramural games (3v3 and 4v4) and practices. These sessions will give young players the chance to develop their ability to dribble, shoot, pass, and receive in a fun and fast-paced format. All the major soccer organizations in the world (USA Soccer, Massachusetts Youth Soccer, and FIFA) recommend small-sided intramural games as the most effective approach for young players to learn to love and succeed in the beautiful game of soccer.

Why 3v3 and 4v4 Are Better for Skill Development Than Typical League Play:
- Require players to figure and participate in the key patterns of soccer: triangle play, 1v1, 2v2, etc.
- Require players to both defend and attack.
- Improve player concentration because ball is close to them at all times.
- The dynamic tempo of small-sided games improves fitness.
- Small-sided games are played without goalies, which increases the number of goals scored and thrills experienced by young players.
- Rules are simplified, emphasizes imaginative play, and promotes growth and appreciation of the game.

In comparison, those few children from Springfield who participated in out-of-school programming attended a YMCA program (see "Springfield YMCA: Program Description").

The difference between these programs is substantial. The mission of the soccer program is to systematically develop soccer players through deliberate practice. The Y program seeks to provide a safe and interactive environment where children can do homework and play with friends in an organized activity, and also serve as a community resource for parents who need affordable child care.

A fourth factor in mastering a skill, and perhaps the most important one, is helping youth develop the desire to achieve. Excellence in performance across domains, including school, requires a great deal of "de-

Springfield YMCA: Program Description

The YMCA of Greater Springfield is committed to the provision of quality, affordable child care and believes that our staff serve as an extension of your family. The children participate in a safe, constructive indoor and outdoor environment which fosters healthy growth and development.

Programming consists of daily activities and relationships that include character development, homework support, literacy, arts and humanities, science and technology, service learning and conflict resolution.

The Dunbar Community Center and YMCA of Greater Springfield have partnered for a NEW before and after school program!

School's Out

School dismissal—4:00 pm	Arrival, homework support, activity centers, snack
4:00–5:30 pm	Main activity period—activity choices
5:30–6:00 pm	Cleanup, quiet activities, departures

Both Breakfast Club and School's Out are designed to allow the children the opportunity to relax and have fun!

liberate practice" over a very long span of time. As previously noted, development in any arena requires challenging oneself, taking risks, making errors, and experiencing frustration, but also involves moving forward and enjoying the sense of accomplishment that comes from mastering what once seemed impossible. To commit oneself to an achievement trajectory requires a great deal of energy and perseverance. Perhaps this commitment, more than anything, will determine whether an individual achieves success. Critical to this process is the desire to engage, be guided, challenge oneself, persevere, and overcome frustration. It also entails developing a love for the process and accepting the subordination of immediate gratification for more durable longer-term outcomes.

The last element relates to Sebastian's observation—"What will these kids be like when they get to our age?" His implied hunch is that if you're good at a young age—receiving coaching, time to play, and positive feedback on your performance and identity—over time you will improve. It's a multiplier effect. Skills beget skills, which suggests that these young people will continue to develop as soccer players. In addition, there is also an emerging research base suggesting that focused commitment to an endeavor—whatever the activity—results in generalizable development of willpower and commitment.

Research scientist Roy Baumeister and *New York Times* science columnist John Tierney review the scientific literature on exercising self-control, will, and resisting temptation in their book *Willpower*. They conclude: "Exercising self-control in one area seemed to improve all areas of life."[5] Charles Duhigg concludes the same in his book *The Power of Habit*, which examines the science of habit formation and performance and its application to individuals and organizations.[6] He quotes Dartmouth research scientist Todd Heatherton to emphasize the ancillary benefit of long-term commitment toward getting good at something:

> That's why signing kids up for piano lessons or sports is so important. It has nothing to do with creating a good musician or a five-year-old soccer star. When you learn to force yourself to practice for an hour or run fifteen laps, you start building self-regulatory strength. A five-year-old who can follow the ball for ten minutes becomes a sixth grader who can start his homework on time.[7]

In other words, the discipline and habits learned while pursuing expertise in one domain transfer to how one shapes and pursues other goals.

HOW THESE PROGRAMS TEACH WHAT IT TAKES TO BE AN EXPERT

Irrespective of which program we visited, we saw actively engaged and enthusiastic adults helping youth grow and develop by sharing their zest for the activity. For example, George Polsky, the executive director of StreetSquash, still moves with alertness and engages in fast-twitch interactions that leave you sensing that on the squash court, he was fluid and panther-like as a standout collegiate and international player. When he walks onto the court, he exudes a sense of comfort that youth palpably feel. This is George's domain; he is a champion squash player. When you walk through the Artists for Humanity building with Susan Rodgerson to meet her staff, you feel as if you are on a reality show of working artists; they dress and carry themselves with aesthetic pizzazz. The artistic staff are indeed practicing artists. When you walk through Zumix, the adults who are not engaged directly with youth are riffing on their instruments or on their mixing consoles.

One of our first and most profound insights into these programs was that they didn't teach *about* squash, or art, or music. They *did* squash, art, and music. And by doing the activity, young people were engaged in the process of acquiring expertise, including practicing, giving and receiving feedback, acquiring habits of self-monitoring and regulation, and learning how to work through failure and success. In short, the youth who partici-pated were undergoing a mind-shaping and habit-structuring experience. Elliot Eisner, a Stanford professor whose writing on how teaching and learning in the arts shapes our ability to understand and make sense of our daily life, contends that

> the human mind is a kind of cultural invention. To be sure chil-dren come into the world well wired, but how they develop, which aptitudes are cultivated and which are left to atrophy, what modes of thinking they become good at are all influenced by the culture in which they reside . . . Thus, the features of the culture to which the child will be exposed and the manner in which the child will address the culture are the most powerful indicators of the kind of thinking and therefore the kind of mind a child is likely to develop during the course of childhood.[8]

In other words, the youth in these programs were absorbed in a culture infusing them with the mentality and habits geared to becoming expert.

To be transparent, we should note that we were expecting some-thing different when we first began our work. We anticipated visiting programs while carrying a figurative butterfly net. Our "prey" would be explicit curricular approaches aimed at developing particular assets identified by the youth development literature as crucial for positive growth. We were well read in the scholarly literature and knew our way around many of the core frameworks that defined the field. We visited organizations and conducted interviews where we had prepared questions like, How do you teach grit? How do you introduce young people to the idea of self-regulation? And how do you then monitor their development in this arena?

We quickly learned both from our own clumsy attempts to explicitly teach these complex capacities in Project Coach and from the polite, but impatient, retorts from practitioners that these capacities, while the lifeblood of these programs, don't get taught methodically or didactically. The programs that we observed—StreetSquash, Artists for Humanity, G-Row, and others—infuse learning, teaching, and socialization into the process of engaging in the activity. This doesn't mean that they ignore or discount the importance of explicitly focusing on "principles of youth development" or academic outcomes; in fact, the programs incorporate contributions from a range of human development research literatures, including prevention, resilience, protective factors, and positive psychology, in an effort to support a young person's social, educational, and personal development.

As a way to understand how all this fits together, meet Destiny Sims, a Dominican woman who grew up in Dorchester, a community in Boston (about a hundred miles from Smith College) that closely resembles the North End of Springfield. Destiny's mother was always worried about her safety while going to and from school or other activities. Like her counterparts from the western part of the state, Destiny's family struggled financially, lived in areas hampered by gang activity, and attended schools that labored to meet state performance standards and to keep kids from dropping out.

Yet, Destiny is a success story. She not only traveled a long distance to get to Smith College, but also graduated in May 2010. Destiny was able to marshal the resources to track a very different trajectory than thousands of her peers. Why did Destiny reach "escape velocity" while the majority of others like her do not?

From our perspective, defying the demographic odds entails many factors. In addition to meeting basic needs for safety and health, it's important for youth to engage in activities that promote an assortment of skills, develop conceptual and practical knowledge, and acquire social capital that can lay the foundation for continued support. They also need to begin forming identities that they themselves value and perceive to be respected by their peers. Such identities must have trajectories connected to paths that lead to positive futures within the mainstream.

But we also are learning that to be successful in such pursuits, knowledge acquisition alone is not sufficient. Youth must be able to ask the right questions, develop strategies for addressing them, have the capacities to find and assess data, and use information to resolve problems. It is important for them to work collaboratively with a diverse range of people. Moreover, they need to be reliable, industrious, emotionally balanced, attentive to detail, willing to persevere in the face of adversity, and able to communicate effectively.

The remainder of the book explores how the framework for getting good at something guides the logic of activities selected and how they are organized and run. The programs do not construct a linear curriculum, but rather establish an operating gestalt focused on success, growth, development, and enjoyment. The founders who embody the spirit of these programs began their work to enable young people to experience what it feels like to master a specific activity. It is a process that includes the following:

- First, young people become enveloped in a *community of practice.* What makes these programs distinctive is that they surround young people with an array of support, opportunity, and resources that enable their growth toward expertise.
- Second, the ethos and practices within the programs foster ways of thinking and behaving that keep young people on the path to success. The programs implicitly and explicitly teach the *mastery mindset.*

- Third, the programs are places where young people discover and experience genuine *intrinsic motivation*. As voluntary programs, they cannot mandate that youth participate, but they provide young people with opportunities to belong, develop competence, and derive satisfaction from being in a community devoted to a particular activity.
- Fourth, the programs recognize that young people need to both build intense bonds within their group and expand their networks to include different groups and associations. The programs provide myriad opportunities for young people to enhance their *social capital*.
- Last, the programs provide the structure and systems to teach supercognitives. However, they also recognize that *transfer of skills* does not happen osmotically, but must be deliberately cultivated across contexts.

In sum, the disparity on the soccer field that struck Sebastian is a snapshot of the systemic differences in opportunity that exist in America and seem to have become more fixed over time.[9] To paraphrase David Brooks, no one knows for sure how to plot a path out of the bottom, but what we need to do is create "thick ecosystems of positive influences" that envelop youth from morning to night.[10] In essence, this is exactly what the principles on expertise, applied to a much narrower array of skills, tell us. We need to inspire youth to take a different path, provide them with the human and material resources to be successful, get them "back on the rails" when things go awry, and keep them going for the mythical ten thousand hours! This, in a nutshell, is what programs are striving to do. The good news is that, although not simple, this is exactly what is being done.

CHAPTER THREE

Communities of Practice

Absorbed in Achieving

A ll the founders that we observed began their program with an image of youth animated and thriving by the sheer exhilarating power of being engaged in their program's core activity. These leaders believed in the transformative power of the journey of getting good at something, be it squash, lacrosse, crew, art, music, or coaching. None of the founders we interviewed had read Reed Larson's important work on the psychology of youth development, and yet the two core themes he articulates resonate through their work.[1] First, he emphasizes, "A central question of youth development is how to get adolescents' fires lit." This speaks to the primal force of motivation. How do you get young people engaged, absorbed, and committed to something? The founders mostly believed that their activity was compelling and that kids would naturally be drawn to it. Once kids came on board and picked up a lacrosse stick, or experienced the thrill of feeling their oars cut through still river waters, they would learn how to learn. In the process, the second element of Larson's dictum would come into play: "develop the complex of dispositions and skills needed to take charge of their lives."

To the founders, it all seemed obvious. Surely, they thought, underserved kids would jump at the chance to play lacrosse or squash, row, or do any of the activities they themselves found so intrinsically captivating. And once kids experienced the euphoria of that activity, they would be hooked and want to stick with it.

Not so fast! As we have seen so often, ideas that strike adults as thoroughly rational and logical don't resonate in the same fashion with youth.

When Zack Lehman decided to start a lacrosse program in Boston, he was sure that kids from Dorchester would flock to the sport. At the time he launched the program in 2000, lacrosse was (and it still is) the fastest-growing team sport in America. Those who play lacrosse call it "mesmerizing"; the *New York Times* describes it as the "fastest sport on two feet." The allure is that the "game is the mix of the best attributes of all sports . . . It has grace, finesse, contact and is a lot of fun to play and watch. People become addicted to it."[2] Yet despite the meteoric growth of lacrosse in the suburbs of Boston, the first years of MetroLacrosse in Dorchester faced formidable challenges. Children there were not inclined to sign up to participate in something they had never seen in their neighborhood and did not understand.

Margot Zalkind worked with several of the key civic and educational leaders in Springfield, Massachusetts, to bring the sport of crew to the city. Every young person growing up in Springfield is aware of the broad, powerful sweep of the Connecticut River. The idea of recruiting Springfield youth to embrace the river felt like a natural story—if only they had the equipment, a boathouse, coaches, and a nudge to get involved in the sport. Surely it would take off. Margot worked out grants with U.S. Rowing, the national YMCA, and other local groups to launch a program. She had the support of community leaders and the mayor of Springfield, and was able to buy some top-notch gear from Concept 2 to get things started. After some initial enthusiasm on the part of a small number of kids, she found it was difficult to grow the numbers and sustain those who had initially joined the program. "We have some great kids, but they just don't seem all that interested in the crew part," she explained. "Crew is hard work and they get interested for a bit, but it's hard to get them to stay."

Evidently, the core activity's novelty interested some kids, but a program's success cannot be explained by simply attributing it to the intrinsic pull of activities. Perhaps a better way to understand the complex dynamics of how these programs get started, grow, and evolve can be found by standing in the lobby of StreetSquash on almost any afternoon. Waiting in the foyer, one can see the crisp, white courts—each named after a legendary Ivy League squash coach or player. The area is designed with sleek contemporary lines. The reception desk is blond wood and the background walls are sharp white, brought into relief with chrome. The space could serve as the entrance to a trendy art gallery—except that it is routinely crawling with youth and their equipment. To walk into StreetSquash is to be confronted by the high energy of teens bantering among themselves and with staff. Watching them congregate inside the lobby reminds one of watching toddlers open presents during the holidays. The wrapping paper and the boxes hold more allure than the actual present itself. As one staff member says, "We have a multimillion facility, beautiful courts, and if we didn't ride herd on the kids, they would be content to chatter away here with each other and with us."

On cue, another staff member uses her "coach voice" and starts to mush kids toward the courts and the classroom. Once inside the classroom, the kids drop their flashy gear bags on the floor and kick their white squash sneakers up on the table. The bantering does not stop—in fact, the chirpy, playful interplay intensifies. I lean over and ask one of the players, "Is it always like this?" He grins and says, "Yeah, it's like the warm-up before a team match begins. Everybody is goofing around and then we get serious."

The young man's observation captured the fundamental and driving force at the heart of these organizations. A program's theme, which appears to most outside observers as its raison d'être, is only tangential to its main purpose, which is to create a framework around which youth can bond with each other and with the staff—whose real goal is youth development. The "advertised activity" might be the headline, but the essence of the story involves the social bonds, and the supportive frameworks are arguably more important than the core activity in reinforcing the initial attraction, and are surely more important in sustaining a youth's involvement. The implicit, and sometimes explicit, message to participants and their families: "If you participate in our program, you will learn what it takes to get good at something that is fun, and in the process acquire skills that transfer to schoolwork and everything else that you do. As well, as a group, we will enjoy the process, support one another, and make it to college together." Consequently, we think that founders initially overestimated the power of the core activity in attracting and sustaining a participant's interest, and underestimated the power of community. The saying "how we do one thing is how we do everything" is a core premise of these programs in that they implicitly believe that a passion for learning in one domain will transfer to others, but the support of a strong and cohesive group is essential to make this happen.

AUDACIOUS MISSIONS: TRYING TO DO THE IMPOSSIBLE

In short, programs like StreetSquash aspire to draw in young people who live on the margins of society, and provide space for fun and play. But they are also serious about the core and driving mission of the work. A quick review of the mission statements of the organizations highlight their aspiration to help young people reinvent themselves and become architects of their own future:

- Project Coach "develops leadership skills and promotes generalizable assets in youth coaches that can be transferred to school, employment, relationships, and other community endeavors."
- Artists for Humanity's mission is to bridge economic, racial, and social divisions by providing "underserved urban youth with the keys to long-term economic and personal self-sufficiency through paid employment in the arts."
- G-Row Boston "uses rowing to teach . . . girls of all cultures, backgrounds, and abilities the importance of relationships, the benefits of exercise, and the power they have to create a positive future for themselves."
- Zumix's mission is to empower "youth who use music to make strong positive change in their lives, their communities, and the world."
- MetroLacrosse's mission is to address the social and economic disparities that exist in urban settings by inspiring personal, ed-

ucational, and athletic success among urban youth and teens. It "teaches youth to take an active role in ensuring their own success in life."

- StreetSquash's mission is to "provide consistent, long-term and reliable support to the children, families and schools in Harlem and Newark. By exposing these children to a broad range of experiences and by maintaining the highest standards, StreetSquash aims to help each child realize his or her academic and personal potential."

In reading through these mission statements, one is struck by their bold, holistic, and all-encompassing reach. Even as gaps and inequities rise in regard to income, education, and life chances, these programs view their mission as promoting equity and opportunities for underserved children and families. As one director said, "We may be trying to do the impossible, but we're trying." This type of gritty aspiration marks all the programs we spent time with over the years researching this book.

The commitment to the larger goals of opportunity and promise remind us of what Jim Collins and Jerry Porras identified in their research of highly successful organizations as a BHAG—a Big Hairy Audacious Goal. A BHAG is "clear and compelling and serves as a unifying focal point of effort—often creating immense team spirit."[3]

The audacity of these goals would occasionally crystallize during observations of the programs in action. For example, one sweltering summer afternoon at the Abe Bashara Boathouse in Lawrence, Massachusetts, during a training session that Project Coach was running for a summer rowing program, we were watching fourteen teenagers examine a long, polished scull. These kids—mostly Dominican and Puerto Rican immigrants—were from Lawrence, a small city of 76,000 north of Boston that once was a flourishing industrial center, but for the last decades had fallen on hard times. They attended schools that graduate just over 50 percent of their students after five years. In fact, Lawrence's schools have floundered for so long that in a historic move in 2011, the state Board of Elementary and Secondary Education voted to place Lawrence schools into receivership in hope of reversing years of dismal academic performance at most of its twenty-eight schools. The vote marked the first time the state had ever fully taken over a school district's finances and academic programs.

On the dock, as the majestic Merrimack River swept by, we watched the group working over the scull—examining it with the same fascination that car buffs would scrutinize a classic restored Mustang. The banter was about 2k erg times and upcoming events. A hulking broad-shouldered young man walked over and joined the discussion. He had grown up crewing in Boston and then in prep school and now crewed for the Boston University varsity team. He volunteered to work in the program as a mentor. A couple of middle-aged men sporting Sperry topsiders, salmon-colored shorts, and flipped up collars joined the conversation. It's frankly rare to see such a diverse group of people interacting in any American context; this group encompassed old, young, middle-aged, black, white, tan, high-income, low-income, fit and unfit, and more.

We were standing on the veranda taking this all in with Ellen Minzner, the director of the program. As a competitor, Minzner was a two-time world champion rower, winning back-to-back gold medals in 1995 and 1996 at the World Rowing Championships. She won gold at the Pan-American Games and set an unofficial world record in 1995. She was an eight-time National Champion and a five-time winner of the Head of the Charles in lightweight coxed eights. After retiring from competition, she was an assistant coach at Kansas State University and the University of California–Berkeley. She is the founder not only of this program but also of other initiatives that try to use sport, and in particular crew, to leverage transformation in the lives of young people. "It's not the crew and the boats and the water, it's this," she says, pointing to the group below, which is still absorbed in a discussion about the scull. "This interaction and this community that forms around these kids is what is important. It's not merely boats and the river. The magic happens because of this."

At Artists for Humanity, we observed a similar quality of spirit; the young people and staff belonged to something distinctive, bounded, and cohesive. One young artist, at work creating a large canvas of a space landscape with soaring meteors arcing into the cosmos, offered perhaps the most cogent synthesis. He painted as we talked and at one point he lifted his paintbrush and said, "We"—he paused with his paintbrush hovering over the canvas—"are Artists for Humanity. We belong here—together."

All around him there were other teenagers holding paintbrushes and palettes. Some sat in front of large canvases; others worked in front of easels and smaller frames. Most of the teenagers were working by themselves—often wearing headphones or earbuds. Interspersed were clumps of teenagers and adults standing before a canvas, talking together. The communal focus emanating from the room bound "this galaxy together" around art making.

The sustained intensity, meaningful activity, and sense of common enterprise may be the defining features of the organizations we examined. One might be tempted to look out among the rows of artisans and think, "this is an art program," but that would discount the true, driving, audacious goal of Artists for Humanity, which is to promote social justice by teaching underserved kids how to become self-sufficient from what they learn as commercial artists in training.

We believe that the notion of community of practice provides a structure for better understanding the interlocking relationship between the core activity at the heart of these organizations and their larger mission to close the achievement gaps and prepare underserved young people to flourish in college and beyond.

COMMUNITIES OF PRACTICE: ENGAGING TOGETHER IN COMMON PURSUITS

It sounds like the lead-in for a bad riddle: "What does an insurance claims processing unit have in common with a youth squash or music program?" Although vastly different in specifics, the work of cognitive anthropologists Jean Lave and Etienne Wenger provides us with a theoretical lens to understand the forces of development at work in the youth organizations we examined.[4]

Wenger's study of the workers of Alinsu Insurance and how they process claims, speak with each other, follow and break procedure, and solve—both alone and together—the steady stream of medical claims problems provides a framework to understand how participation in organizations like StreetSquash, Artists for Humanity, and Project Coach can help some young people move forward with their lives. Wenger's overarching premise is that learning and growing happen when we interact with each other and engage in common pursuits.[5] It builds on his work with Jean Lave, which examines how people learn and grow within communities where participants are engaged in real activities that require skills, development, and ongoing learning. Their research offers a competing framework to what Lave sees as traditional schooling's end goal of the "internalization of knowledge by individuals." She quite elegantly captures the difference between these two approaches to learning: "Developing an identity as a member of a community and becoming knowledgeably skillful are part of the same process, with the former motivating, shaping, and giving meaning to the latter, which it subsumes."[6] Furthermore, she elaborates that in a community of practice, "learning, thinking, and knowing are relations among people engaged in activity in, with, and arising from the socially and culturally structured world."[7]

Lave argues that learning is a by-product of participating in a community rather than a discrete and independent entity that exists separate from "culture, history and the social world," as it may be for youth in underresourced and dysfunctional schools.[8] Lave and Wenger extend the idea that robust knowledge and understandings are fundamentally social phenomena and that we may learn best when interacting around problems that are meaningful. They call this interaction a community of practice, which they describe as groups of people who share an interest or commitment to a practice and regularly work together.

Through membership in a community and engaging in regular and routine activities, a community of practice develops ways of doing things, views of the world, values, power relations, modes of discourse, and identities. Thus, who we are develops through our daily interactions within that community, and also with those outside of it. So when a youth talks about how belonging to Artists for Humanity makes her feel like an artist, it is because of the complex interactions taking place between the feelings she has in the studio with a paintbrush in her hand and the sense of self she derives from talking with a business client who treats her as an artist. To Lave and Wenger, these communities of practice work because they make organic connections among practice, social relationships, and identity formation that promote learning that becomes authentically embedded in one's intellectual, emotional, and social life.

For the programs that we observed, the outcome of participation is not only about acquiring practical knowledge and know-how, but also about developing an identity as a member of these communities. Engaging in these programs changes who the youth are, creates personal histories of success, and launches visions of possible futures quite different from those presumed prior to joining. As Wenger writes, "Education, in its deepest sense and at whatever age it takes place, concerns the opening of our identities—exploring new ways of being that lie beyond our current state. Whereas training aims to create an inbound trajectory targeted at competence at a specific practice, education must strive to open new dimensions for the negotiation of the self . . . Education is not merely formative—it is transformative."[9]

While an in-depth, technical examination of the notion of community of practice goes beyond the scope of this book, the essential ideas associated with it are easily understood by most people who have participated in such communities. Artists, academics, musicians, chess players, computer engineers, and athletes all seek out communities in which they feel as if they belong because they are populated by like-minded people, and in which they can acquire knowledge and skills that would be incrementally more difficult to gain on their own.

We believe that the best out-of-school organizations contain the same elements as those found in such communities. We next describe their core elements.

THE STRUCTURE OF COMMUNITIES OF PRACTICE

To more fully appreciate the multifaceted mission that becomes the "spirit" of these communities of practice, it is useful to more fully examine the structure of a community of practice. Wenger posits that communities of practice have three distinct features. First, they have an identity defined by a shared domain of interest. Membership therefore implies a commitment to the domain and a shared passion for an activity that distinguishes members from other people. Second, they have a community. In pursuing their interest in their domain, members engage in joint activities and discussions, help one another, and share information. They build relationships that enable them to learn from each other and derive a powerful sense of belonging from participation. Third, a community of practice is not merely a community of interest in the abstract; members of a community of practice are active and engaged practitioners. They develop a shared repertoire of resources: experiences, stories, tools, ways of addressing recurring problems—in short, a shared practice. This takes time and sustained interaction.

The Domain

A domain is the endeavor that draws participants together. For a sports program such as StreetSquash, this could entail developing greater skill, fulfilling a competitive schedule, competing successfully against others, and/or playing in an intramural sports league. For Artists for Humanity this could mean soliciting and fulfilling the specifications for a commission for completing a mural, crafting a sculpture, or designing a bicycle rack. This would also entail gaining new understandings about art and acquiring the skills to produce something that has aesthetic appeal and meets the technical specifications of a buyer. Likewise, for Zumix, the domain centers on learning, making, and producing music, whether for oneself or as a commodity that can be commissioned.

The essence of domain is the core activity and the major reason for having a group of individuals come together. In the out-of-school literature, the notion of domain seems synonymous with the term *hook* in that it is what captures the imagination and passion of the participants. The domain is synonymous with a group's reason for being, and is usually the first descriptor staff use when explaining their programs to potential participants, their families, school administrators, and funders. While all domains have unique qualities, and certainly their share of advocates, we have come to see them more as "placeholders" to attract and sustain a youth's interest over time than as entities with magical transformative powers in themselves. Whether or not involvement in a domain really enhances the developmental trajectory of youth has much more to do with their day-to-day experiences than anything inherent in the activity itself.

The Community or Tribe

The community element entails having a sense of belonging to the group and developing a complex web of social relationships that binds one to the group. For adolescents struggling to solidify their sense of self and understand themselves in relation to others in their social world, the character of these organizations as communities is fundamental. Participants come together because of a shared interest in the domain, but they become knitted together by what Preskill and Torres describe as "matters of heart as well as the mind" into something that is almost tribal.[10]

Seth Godin, the author of *Tribes: We Need You to Lead Us* and other books that routinely sit atop the best-seller list, synthesizes a vast corpus of psychological, sociological, and evolutionary research when he writes, "Human beings can't help it: we need to belong. One of the most powerful of our survival mechanisms is to be part of a tribe, to contribute to (and take from) a group of like-minded people . . . we can't resist the rush of belonging."[11]

The "rush of belonging" manifests itself in a myriad of ways in the programs we studied. Whenever the young people talked about their participation in programs, they repeatedly described their affiliation as "my squash family," "my posse," "my sanctuary," "my people," or "my team." These communities of practice were not just clinical or sanitized settings where young people were exposed to the rudiments of an activity, but settings that provided them with intensive, immediate experiences that were enjoyable, challenging, and charged with the social complexity that authentically attracted their attention. They also implicitly held the promise of long-term personal benefits.

In a much-cited article, psychologists Roy Baumeister and Mark Leary put forth what they describe as the "belonging" hypothesis, which contends that humans have a pervasive drive to form and maintain lasting, positive, and significant interpersonal relationships.[12] Satisfying this drive involves two criteria: "First, there is a need for frequent, affectively pleasant interactions with a few other people, and, second, these interactions must take place in the context of a temporally stable and enduring framework of affective concern for each other's welfare."[13] In other words, frequent contact with others who care about and value you as a person provides the mortar to cement the bricks of personhood together and build a community of practice.

This was vividly illustrated for us when a community leader from the neighborhood where we work asked if he could speak to Project Coach. A theme running through our coach development that year had been the exploration of the two motives of leadership: service to others or belittling of others. It was a theme that resonated with our coaches—often charismatic, high-status youth in the circles they moved in—who were faced with the ongoing choice: how will I use my influence?

We had heard Manny talk about his personal reformation from gang leader to community leader. He was a commanding and charismatic presence at community meetings and he knew about Project Coach because his own children were players in our league.

When Manny came to talk, his Yankee hat was pitched to the side and he was dripping with sweat—so much so that he constantly dabbed himself with a small towel. His oversized shirt barely covered his thickly muscled arms and a neck bejeweled with several heavy gold chains. He exuded energy, aggression, passion, and fervor. As he delivered his speech, he never stopped stalking around the classroom.

> I needed an addiction. I needed to feel good at something. I needed to belong to something. I did it the wrong way. My brother died because we did evil. He ended up murdered— dead on the street. I hurt people and did things I can't think about, but you are doing it the right way. You belong to your own gang. The Project Coach gang . . . You got each other and sometimes you do things that make a difference. You help kids out and that's the most important

because kids are our future. I look back now at all I did and all that I wasted. I have regrets. I didn't know better. I didn't see the options and now so many knuckleheads are out there doing the same thing that I did and even worse. It's even worse out there.

Manny's talk was raw. He talked for forty-five minutes, his speech full of F bombs and graphic images of horrific violence. He spoke from the heart, and our youth listened with reverence and respect because they knew him and his reputation. He was real to them. At one point he pulled off his Yankee hat and stared out at the twenty-five or so assembled teens staring back at him. In that moment, you could feel this outpouring of complex feelings. He said, "I wish I would have done things differently. I could have been different. You have this chance." When Manny finished, he bowed his head, paused, and then said, "You have each other. You have to stick with each other." His conclusion lifts up an enduring attribute of the human condition that helps us understand the nature of these communities—they tap into a young person's fundamental and compelling need to belong to something. Peer associations provide companionship, support, and intimacy. They are necessary for successful development. He was asking, in essence, who are your people? What tribe do you belong to?

The Role of Staff in a Community of Practice

A group within these communities of practice is the staff. As a cohort, the staff in the programs we examined resembled the program founders more than they did the participants. Many had also participated in the program domain in one way or another throughout their lives, including during college—often colleges ranked as selective. Another subset of staff had little, if any, domain-specific expertise, but had also attended similar selective colleges and served in positions such as academic advisor, advancement director, or college advisor. A common thread among all these individuals was that they were young, enthusiastic, intelligent, and idealistic. From a community of practice perspective, one can see how having such people in the mix brings a level of energy and expertise to the youth and academic development aspects of programs. Such staff can do "the talk" because they have done "the walk." They serve not only as coaches, teachers, and mentors but also as models of people who realized their aspirations by making wise choices, working hard, and connecting with the right people. Consistent with the notion of community of practice, staff have a very different sort of relationship with youth than do teachers, or even parents. From our interviews with participants and staff, it appeared to us that staff served a variety of roles, including friend, advocate, coach, tutor, mentor, and repository of procedural knowledge.

As programs mature, some graduates return to assume leadership roles. Such individuals typically take on a missionary's zeal as they can explicitly connect the dots from where they were to what they have become, and they understand how engaging in the program provided the glue, inspiration, and resources for their new life trajectories. In our experience, these individuals are among the best recruiters, instructors, and mentors.

While we have come across many such individuals in our travels, we immediately think of Jonny Lopez, who started with us as a fifth grader. At that time, he participated as a player in our twice-weekly sports sessions. When he moved on to sixth grade and was too old to be a player, we took him on as an assistant coach, where he helped out as needed. When he got to eighth grade, we hired him as a paid coach, and he continued in this capacity throughout high school. Upon graduating, he enrolled at a local community college, and we created a new supervisory position that entails overseeing the work of high school coaches and leading selected classes and activities at our weekly coaching academy. Jonny also roves about and interacts with younger kids. Individuals like Jonny are not only well-trained staff, but also powerful symbols that Project Coach values such people and will support their development along the way. This is clearly a win-win enterprise in which programs are strengthened by developing a cadre of caring and committed members, and the individuals themselves acquire knowledge and skills that can be leveraged in other venues. Indeed, Jonny also serves in a supervisory capacity in another program located in a nearby middle- to upper-class suburb. To think that little Jonny, whom we knew as a fifth grader living in a very challenged urban community, is now working with us, serving as a leader in a much more resourced community, all while going to college, seems quite remarkable.

Besides program staff, there are the people who run and maintain the program facilities. Often these people are invisible to outside observers and evaluators who track logic diagrams and attempt to determine relationships between activities and outcomes. However, Nataha, a StreetSquasher, told us that when her peers have personal problems, some of their favorite people to talk to are James, the building custodian, or Shade, the front desk monitor. She explained that though such folks may seem removed from the main mission of the program, they too are an important part of the entire enterprise. In Project Coach we have Wilfredo, who serves as our dismissal guard; he grew up in the neighborhood where we work and can connect in a different way with kids and families than the staff who live in other locales. Such support staff are critical to the day-to-day operations of communities of practice and should not be undervalued.

In our travels, we also came across other individuals who are part of the community. We have seen volunteer tutors—generally college students who work with participants on a weekly basis. Many programs also recruit adult mentors who connect with participants in domain and non-domain-specific activities on a monthly basis. Members of boards may also meet with kids at less regular intervals. We learned to appreciate all the different types of people within organizations, the distinctive roles that they play, and the intricate webs of relationships that form to promote a program's central mission.

Practice

From the domain and community comes "the practice," which has the same connotation as when a physician, lawyer, or teacher is licensed to practice. Individuals who are part of these communities acquire knowledge and skills both explicitly and implicitly through the anecdotes, experiences, shared activities, meetings, and formal classes to which participants are exposed. The uniqueness of this aggregate gives a group a discrete character, and individuals within it a distinct identity. When we attended the urban national squash championships, in which ten programs affiliated with the National Urban Squash and Education Association participated, we were struck by the pride that players and staff took in conveying who they were and what they represented. For example, on a board that posted the creative writings of competitors, we saw an essay by Darryl Washington, who was identified as U13 and represented Racquet Up, a Detroit affiliate:

> One of my teammates Jerreon was struggling playing squash. You see, Jerreon was having trouble with his serves. So I just told him to open his racquet more and watch the ball at all times. He tried it and he made it seem like he was a professional squash player. His game started getting better and better every time he got on court.

On a posting from Carlos Marks, also identified as U13 and representing SquashWise, a Baltimore affiliate, he provides advice about developing psychological skills self-talk:

> Telling myself not to give up and keep trying as hard as I can. For an example in a squash match, I was down 7–1; and I talked to myself and said, "I can still win, have confidence." I came back strong and ended up with a score of 11, while my opponent was left with 9.

These practices are explicitly related to the activity. Another more critical element of practice in all the programs we examined has to do with the goal of promoting general success. As one staff member said, "If we're going to help our kids grow and get ready for what is next in their life, we need to provide them with all kinds of learning experiences and opportunities." Their implicit theory of change is to help youth achieve success by wrapping them in support, opportunities, and structure. In some ways, this approach can seem willy-nilly, as one director said:

> We throw everything and the kitchen sink at helping these kids. If they need counseling, we'll try and get it for them. If they need SAT tutoring—done. If they need help on their biology—we find them

a tutor. If they have a problem with a teacher—we'll try and intervene. If they can benefit from a summer experience—we'll arrange it. We do what needs to be done.

As Greg Zaff, the executive director of SquashBusters, said, "We value each kid; no one gets lost in the shuffle. Each is immersed in love, support, and attention. This is what matters most, not squash." Zaff's depiction of his program as a space of "love, support, and attention" is often echoed by participants and their parents. "We are a family" is a refrain we heard from many young people when we asked them to describe what the program meant to them. When we spoke to parents of participants—most of whom were working-class parents without college educations—they almost always described the programs as "helping raise and support" their son or daughter. As one mother said, "They help with homework, school, college, and they keep her busy and occupied, which keeps her out of trouble and moving in a good direction." Another parent said, "When Larisa is at the program, I know they are helping her get her work done and they are watching her like I do."

IN THINKING ABOUT THE overarching mission of these communities of practice, we began to believe that they strive to complement and supplement what busy and often overtaxed parents provide for their children. The programs work hard to be connected and enmeshed with parents, but they also hold a particular view of how they can help young people coming from underserved circumstances. Many out-of-school programs such as StreetSquash, Artists for Humanity, G-Row, and Project Coach, which we frame as communities of practice, are stepping into this void and taking the role as the concerted cultivators of youth who, by default, were following a natural growth trajectory. As Greg Zaff conveyed, these organizations are multidimensional communities that do whatever it takes to support the development of their youth, just as parents and families provide support for their children. They teach kids what it means to work hard and be productive citizens, while providing the necessary personal and financial support for them to realize their aspirations as artists, athletes, musicians, and students. A recent fund-raising e-newsletter from Harlem RBI summarizes the essence of these organizations in showing a picture of a youth pitching a baseball with this caption:

> Meet Nixon. Here he is working on his fastball. But before he wins the Cy Young Award, he will need to eat right, get good grades, graduate from high school and go to college. And we are going to be there for him every step of the way.

Because of these programs, we are seeing the playing field being leveled, and unequal childhoods becoming more equal. Now there is a parallel path for underserved youth to become more competitive with their more privileged peers. Sebastian would be amazed to see kids who look like the ones he coaches and have comparable challenges now playing squash, rowing, producing art, and making music qualitatively indistinguishable from that produced by the suburban kids he had watched in dismay. They are also succeeding academically, finishing high school and being accepted at colleges that only a few years ago seemed beyond reach.

In essence, the practice component of these communities of practice begins with the teaching and sharing of domain-specific elements; then, by embracing other endeavors important to youth, they "concertedly cultivate" achievement across a range of activities. In the next chapter we will explain how these communities of practice help youth to build the intraindividual capacities necessary for competing and succeeding in a world very different from the one in which they live.

CHAPTER FOUR

Learning a Mastery Mindset
The Will to Excel

A s we climbed the stairs of Springfield's City Hall toward the Greek revival columns that stood as stalwarts on the promenade, one of our teen coaches said, "You know a monkey burned this building down?" We swiveled to look at him and he said with a grin, "Yeah, I went on a class trip here and they tell the story about how a monkey knocked a lamp over and the old City Hall burnt down."

We continued talking about monkeys as we ascended the sweeping marble staircase toward room 220, before our presentation to the mayor, the school superintendent, and the Springfield City Council School Committee. This was a big moment for us in Project Coach. We were on the agenda to present our work to the local power brokers. In assembling the presentation we had divided up parts and decided to have one of the teen coaches participate. Loeb was selected as the ambassador of the coaches, and he had written up his comments in preparation for the discussion.

The room was ornate, with gleaming chandeliers, dark and sober paneling, high arching ceilings, and vaulted windows. Aside from the television camera, we felt as if we were stepping back into Springfield's colonial history. This grandiose stage was a bit stressful even to us, adults who had delivered numerous presentations over the years, and we could not help wondering what Loeb was feeling. Walking into the room we were still joking about the monkey, which struck us as in keeping with the spirit of our Project Coach training—it emphasizes how athletes can employ various attentional strategies to control anxiety, which may hinder optimal performance. Monkey talk distracted all of us from the solemnity of the proceedings, and helped us remain calm prior to being called.

We were finally summoned to the podium. Our presentation began with an overview of our work. After the adults had finished, we turned it over to Loeb. He rose hesitantly, his wide eyes darting around the room, but then he regrouped and moved confidently to the lectern. Loeb introduced himself, paused, and began:

> I can name many ways Project Coach has helped me, but the two biggest would have to be building self-confidence in what I am doing, and helping me to see a clear and brighter future, and that I could strive to be a better student and mentor to others. Project Coach began an education initiative, which slowly motivated me to do better in school. I had a previous GPA of less than a 1.9 and I am very proud to say that I graduated senior year with a 3.0 after working hard with Greg—our academic director—and student tutors and mentors from Smith College. I also learned how to work with my teachers better so that they understood me more, and how to find help when I needed it. In my opinion Project Coach was one of the biggest things to ever happen to the North End. It teaches kids in our neighborhood to look outside of their problems at home and focus on being a better individual, and a positive role model to others.

He finished and the entire assembly rose and applauded. As we watched, we couldn't help but wonder: for Loeb—what changed? What "flipped the switch" for him? What explains his transformation in school? How did becoming a community leader and role model for younger children alter his future aspirations? How could a kid from the long-struggling North End neighborhood have the confidence and capacity to address the mayor, school superintendent, and city council in a televised public forum, and get a standing ovation for his message?

There are myriad ways to interpret and explain Loeb's transformation, but his own reflection says it best:

> I think that I started to grow up and care more about my future. I started to believe in what I could become and once that started, I started to care about my grades because I saw and understood why they were important to my future. I also learned how to get organized and get stuff done and then I had help from the mentors in the program if I needed tutoring. They also texted me and nagged me all the time to get things done.

In this vignette we learn that Loeb first developed new ways of seeing himself, his place in the world, and his future—possibilities vastly different from what he had envisioned in the past. In a sense, such changing perceptions about himself were critical for developing the motivation to learn the necessary technical skills of coaching and leadership, as well as to become more serious and conscientious about his schoolwork. Paul Tough astutely points out that for kids to be successful, they need the proper motivation and the technical know-how. However, the latter without the former is unlikely to produce the desired results.[1] He notes that "if students just aren't motivated to achieve the goals their teachers or parents want them to achieve . . . all the self-control tricks in the world aren't going to help."[2]

From our perspective, understanding how to inspire a youth's motivation to achieve has been a missing element in educational reform movements. So much has been focused on structural elements such as teacher quality, longer days, smaller schools, and standardized testing that we have forgotten what Thorndike told us in his Law of Readiness—that children need to be ready to learn, physically, intellectually, and emotionally, or it just will not happen. For youth like Loeb, something had to provide the spark that lit his fire.

We believe that such a transformation came about for Loeb, and many others like him, from being part of communities that "light these fires." Participating in an assortment of activities with others ensconced in an environment that exudes optimism, personal development, upward mobility, community service, and social justice has a way of changing youth. This significant reframing of participants' mindsets is why these programs do so well and what got Loeb to this forum. Of course, mindset alone was not sufficient for him to become a more proficient coach, inspiring leader, or superior student; developing such skills requires specialized knowledge, practice, and social support. These programs provide these in abundance. However, without the appropriate motivation and mindset to embed such capabilities, it is unlikely that that they would ever be acquired, or manifested.

Consequently, we have come to believe that the emphasis should be on how out-of-school programs shape their participants' identities, mindsets, and ways of thinking. We conclude that when individuals learn to be optimistic, when they begin to understand and seek self–actualization, and when they begin to see futures that are attractive, the challenge of teaching them technical information, thematic skills, or how to succeed in school becomes a natural extension of who they are becoming.[3] As we see it, the key to helping youth thrive is to first get them to think more productively about themselves and the possible worlds in which they could live, and then to support them on a day-to-day basis with whatever is needed to realize their aspirations.

In our observations of programs and, in particular, our many conversations with graduates of these programs, we too saw them as settings intent on providing opportunities for young people to undergo a variety of explicit and implicit experiences aimed at personal identity formation and development. Like Loeb, we heard young adults who participated in these programs tell us stories of how the people and experiences helped them to "aim high," to "get ahead," or, as one recent college graduate said about her time in an organization devoted to political activism and leadership in Boston, "I was always a person with goals even though that wasn't what everybody in my school and neighborhood had, and the staff and all the experiences at New Hyde helped me stay focused and encouraged me to do my best."

In hearing such reflections and triangulating them with the written materials published by programs and our interviews with staff, we began to understand the particular kind of personal development that was occurring. As an aggregate, this development focused on participants' acquiring a set of habits, dispositions, and qualities that paralleled what Larson describes as getting adolescents' "fire lit" and then helping them to acquire the array of assets that would help them to be successful in future endeavors.[4] This also dovetails with what Lareau frames as "concerted cultivation" in her studies of the child-rearing habits of middle-class parents who assiduously work to foster their child's capabilities by making certain that they are exposed to a variety of engaging and enriching experiences.[5] In essence, these programs cultivated the same attributes in participants that allowed their more privileged peers to gain differential advantages in the way they understood themselves, related to one another, communicated with adults, interacted with the institutions in their lives, and thought about their futures.

In considering Loeb's case, he himself recognizes several key elements. First, Project Coach added a predictable structure and routines to his out-of-school life. He had a place to go where he had friends and adults who were supportive of his development as a coach, as a student, and as a person. As well, the schedule was organized to provide him with coach training, coaching time, study hall with tutors, and systems to help him keep his responsibilities cohered and organized.

Over the years that Loeb participated, he gradually began to understand and internalize a prevailing ethos of the program: getting good at anything requires hard work over an extended period of time. As well, he learned that being able to work at something for a long time requires a positive attitude, a willingness to expend effort, a readiness to accept both positive and corrective feedback, and the "grit" to endure when challenges seem to exceed self-perceived capabilities. Such an ethos helped Loeb develop what might be labeled an "achievement mindset"—a manner of thinking about one's present challenges and future aspirations in productive and realistic ways that open up new possibilities. In his appearance with the mayor, school board, and the school superintendent, he also learned that his views counted and that he now had the tools and social capital to influence how powerful decision makers thought about and responded to the things he and his peers valued.

THE IMPORTANCE OF MINDSET

Our sense of how all these elements work together was both confirmed and clarified by a recent monograph by Farrington et al. entitled *Teaching Adolescents to Become Learners: The Role of Noncognitive Factors in Shaping School Performance: A Critical Literature Review.*[6] The report contests current policy efforts that rest on the simple linear assumption that a more rigorous high school curriculum will improve student performance on standardized tests and their ability to compete in a global economy. The report chides this simplistic formula, arguing that "there is little to no rigorous evidence that efforts to increase standards and require higher- level coursework—*in and of themselves*—are likely to lead many more students to complete high school and attain college degrees." Instead, the monograph cites a range of studies that contend that what matters most for college graduation is not test scores or the courses taken by high school students, but their high school grades, which the authors say "are vastly better predictors of high school and college performance and graduation, as well as a host of longer-term life outcomes, than their standardized test scores."[7]

The prevailing interpretation of this observation is that, in addition to measuring students' content knowledge and core academic skills, grades also reflect the degree to which students have demonstrated a range of achievement behaviors. These include an array of attitudes, strategies, and skills that are critical for success in school and in later life. Noted are such things as attendance, deliberate work habits, study skills, time management, help-seeking, metacognitive processes, and academic and social problem-solving skills. These findings make sense. Students who regularly come to class, focus, and complete assigned work have likely developed the kind of work habits that that produce success in high school, in college, and later in the workforce. Students who struggle with self-discipline and are erratic in how they engage in high school classes will likely find the challenges of college overwhelming, regardless of their intellectual ability or content knowledge. The finding that course grades matter more than achievement test scores suggests that grades do indeed capture something important about students that test scores do not. Seemingly, they also reflect such things as their attitudes about learning, their beliefs about their own intelligence, their self-control and persistence, and the quality of their relationships with peers and adults.[8]

Farrington et al. conclude that the education establishment seems to have doubled down on enhancing standardized test scores when it should also be fostering the capacities that promote a more general achievement-oriented mindset. They state that:

> Teaching adolescents to become learners requires more than improving test scores; it means transforming classrooms into places alive with ideas that engage students' natural curiosity and desire to learn in preparation for college, career, and meaningful adult lives. This requires schools to build not only students' skills and knowledge but also their sense of what is possible for themselves, as they develop the strategies, behaviors, and attitudes that allow them to bring their aspirations to fruition.[9]

The takeaway from this research is compelling, and confirms what we learned from leaders in the out-of-school world, and from researchers such as Larson and Lareau. School, just like the programs that we have written about, should focus on providing a "developmental wraparound" for young people so that their work habits and supercognitive capacities can be cultivated, affirmed, and reinforced. Developing the capacities that we have labeled the "achievement mindset" should not be seen as an add-on to the work that educators have been asked to do, but intricately interwoven into their teaching. Indeed, fostering these capacities has been found to produce better students, and does not detract from the time and energy teachers might devote to academic material. The following story about Jason Talbot illustrates how mindset and achievement are intertwined.

JASON TALBOT: BECOMING AN ARTIST

When Jason Talbot walked toward us from across the large painting studio in the Artists for Humanity complex, he exuded an MTV cool. The main painting gallery has nearly seventy-five easels set up in a semblance of lines, and as he picked his way past the working artists, Jason would briefly stop and gaze at a painting or share a quick exchange with a teenager. As with so many of the high-impact leaders we met, he seemed to take every opportunity to connect, share moments, check in, and just basically keep a complex conversation flowing. As we shook his hand, we said, "This is a pretty special place." He answered, "That it is." As we did with almost all of our interviews, we began by asking: How did you come to do the work that you are doing?

Jason's story begins in Martin Luther King Jr. Middle School when Susan Rodgerson invited him to participate in a painting project in the school's library. Jason (now in his midthirties) described himself as a pretty intelligent student who loved to cut up and have fun—albeit one who had an interest in art, particularly graffiti. Over the course of that first project, the team overcame obstacles, shared ideas, and, finally, accomplished their goal. Susan later invited Jason and a small group of his middle school classmates to work with her in her small painting studio in the South End. He described these as art sessions with lots of opportunity for creative expression and replete with the give-and-take that unfolds when teenagers get together. The art making took on momentum, and soon the initial core group was tagging along with Susan when she met with clients to develop creative ventures, pitch projects, and turn art into income. Soon the group developed several projects that involved Jason's special passion for graffiti. As a result, his commitment took on even more significance and promise. In reflecting back on the experience, he said:

> Boston is a college town, it's the hub of commerce, but you have some kids that are totally shut off and segregated from those opportunities and find themselves misguided, with terrible role models. Susan helped us understand that to be successful you had to work hard. That wasn't the message I always received when I was a teenager. We thought to be successful you had to deal drugs, be able to jump high, be a basketball player, or win the lottery.

Art was becoming a way to understand himself, his life, and his future. More importantly, Jason was being acculturated into a mindset and way of living in the world that pivoted on the idea that much is possible if one works hard, attends to details, and keeps at it.

> Susan helped to redirect us, as teenagers, to hard work. She helped us feel welcome in Boston, in arenas like Newbury Street. I didn't feel welcome in the art galleries all up and down Newbury Street. Being a painter and starting to see my work in those places, that's when I started to feel included and that I had an alternative to some of the negative things that were going on in the street.

While producing quality art was its central focus, the group evolved to embody the most central principles of a community of practice. Members began to see themselves as artists and, thus, needed to practice the behaviors of artists. Susan's steady, tenacious presence pushed them and demanded that they conduct themselves with the artistic and professional behaviors that she held for herself and that she knew her clients demanded. Producing high-quality art required hard work, attention to detail, persistence, a commitment to meeting deadlines, and a willingness to be critiqued and revise one's work. In short, Jason was undergoing a heady and transformative course of personal development. In Larson's language, this entailed experiencing, exploring, and expanding one's sense of identity, and engaging in initiative-taking activities that involve expending significant and sustained effort toward achieving meaningful goals.[10]

Within our framework, we see Jason's experience as emblematic of becoming a member of an achievement-oriented community of practice—something happened that we believe is central to the experiences that young people have in these programs. They begin to thrive, expand, and dream. These communities of practice flow in centrifugal patterns and depend on interactive, relational processes that include an aggregate of implicit, explicit, overt, and tacit learning. This is a natural way of learning according to eminent cognitive scientist John Seely Brown, who writes, "Knowing (and not just learning) is inextricably situated in the physical and social context of its acquisition and use. It cannot be extracted from these without being irretrievably transformed."[11] In other words, Artists for Humanity and other such programs provide opportunities for young people to become absorbed in a context where the act of producing something, whether it's a sculpture, a portrait, a forehand, a dance step, or a jump shot, builds a productive sense of self, identity, and impending achievement.

For Jason and for so many others, belonging to their organization and participating in the primary activity triggers exploration and reflection on personal ability, interest, ideals, aspiration, and competence. The interaction of teenagers within a community of practice is a high-stakes encounter that impacts not only how they experience the present, but also the contour and trajectory of their lives going forward. It is about identity, sense of self, role, and place in a social context. Erik Erikson, whose work on identity theory in the 1940s describes the project of seeking a coherent sense of identity as a primary human challenge, explains the fundamental importance of finding a secure identity as akin to finding the "person in personality."[12] Finding and knowing yourself is the crucial challenge of adolescence.

According to Susan Rodgerson:

> Young people come to us because they need a job or a safe place to go after school. They start our training program and it's real and focused on the development of useful art skills and they find success. They don't always feel successful at school; this may be the first success they have tasted in a while and it feels good and important. Once they experience this they start to feel like artists and call themselves artists. They take on the identity of artist.

The structure provided by these programs provides an outlet for young people to try on a story of themselves as a certain kind of person. The youth who feel that glow of accomplishment and sense of belonging to a group are actively constructing a reality for themselves, while also acquiring an array of assets and attitudes that are transferable to other critical parts of their lives.

MINDSETS ARE NOT CREATED IN ISOLATION BUT WITHIN COMMUNITY

Michael Nakkula and Eric Toshalis, researchers who have done important work on how schools can be powerful settings for youth development, assert that "adolescents are in a near-constant state of constructing their lives.[13] Synthesizing a wide range of studies drawn from a myriad of disciplines, they offer a view of youth development that has the features of a story and narrative. People build guiding stories for their lives. They write, "These stories serve to integrate experience across time, and like literary fiction or accounts of world history, they become marked by core themes."[14] These themes reverberate and help give meaning to the present, but also shape the future:

> The construction of one's life, from this perspective, occurs through and gets held together by the evolving stories we tell ourselves and ways in which these stories become internal guideposts for ongoing decision making, everyday behavior and self-understanding . . . Being human requires the authoring of one's life, of one's life story. Having a coherent functional sense of one's self requires ongoing, active engagement in this authoring process.[15]

We do not create our life stories, personal narratives, and mindsets in isolation. Who we are grows out of the connections, the tribes and communities with which we affiliate, and those contexts through which we pass in our everyday lives. In other words, the self-stories and mindsets that guide our life are coauthored by those circles of culture, class, and institutions within which we engage. We believe that the organizations that we focus on in this book have a potent capacity to be coauthors of a young person's life journey by cultivating particular positive and constructive mindsets. As Jason said, "A hammer is a tool. You can use it to hammer in a nail or you can use it to chisel out the statue of David; the difference is the level of creativity possessed by the person swinging that hammer. We cultivate the creativity of our participants, so they can make a brighter future for themselves and their communities."

In thinking about the people and programs that we came to know, it's clear that the effort to contribute to a positive life story begins with cultivating crucial mindsets—personal, social, and cultural. The research of Farkas et al. focuses on exposing and emphasizing the link between skills and behaviors in school, other contexts, and later life outcomes. They contend that "behavior and skills do not develop in a vacuum. Rather their development is driven by a student's . . . attitudes and expectations."[16] These do not spring fully formed or get adopted and worn like a new shirt. They derive from the larger social contexts through which individuals move.

This view dovetails with Lareau's overarching premise that young people develop mindsets and ways of interacting with the world from how their daily lives are organized and how they engage in activities, relate to institutions, and think about themselves. For Lareau, a youth's mindset is shaped by the rhythms of everyday life, which her research contends is linked to social class. The conceptual underpinnings of her findings trace back to the important work of Pierre Bourdieu, who claims that individuals of different social strata are socialized differently.[17] He defines this process as a consequence of being exposed to people with different cultural heritages, knowledge, dispositions, and skills that pass through families, generations, and neighborhood groups. Bourdieau contends that mindsets emerge from the attitudes, beliefs, and experiences people garner from their social world. In other words, the mindsets that shape one's values, aspirations, and attitudes toward one's community, institutions such as school, or future career aspirations are highly related to the people with whom one associates. As Jay Macleod noted in his acclaimed ethnography of youth growing up in New York City:

> A lower-class child growing up in an environment where success
> is rare is much less likely to develop strong ambitions than is a
> middle-class boy or girl growing up in a social world peopled by

those who have "made it" and where the connection between effort and reward is taken for granted.[18]

These dispositions are critical to shaping teenagers' journey to adulthood, which is often defined by such things as success in school and making connections to activities and people that can help them build assets and expand possibilities for what they might become. The impact of such experiences and relationships can be understood at least in part through exploring three mindsets that the programs we came to know attempted to cultivate: embracing college, growth through hard work, and resilience.

POSITIVE SELVES: A MINDSET THAT INCLUDES COLLEGE

In many ways, the programs viewed themselves as a vehicle to transport low-income youth to college. While ambitious in scope, the reality was daunting. Consider, for example, the gap in evidence when our coaches spent the day at a coaching skills workshop focused on games-based soccer coaching. The games-based approach emphasizes play, movement, and teaching technical and tactical skills within the flow of constrained games, whereas the conventional approach might teach a line of kids how to strike and dribble the ball with the proper parts of the foot.

The culminating event of the workshop was for our coaches to put on a clinic for kindergartners and first graders from the town soccer club. We arrived early and arranged the field as the little players began to show up. Each of the youngsters was dressed in soccer shorts, shin pads, and cleats. An inordinate number of them wore shirts decorated with the names and mascots of various highly competitive colleges: Smith College, Amherst College, Stanford, Williams, and several more. At one point, we overheard an exchange between a kindergartner and one of our high school juniors who was following one of the Project Coach protocols: when you meet a player on your team, you should ask her a question. We often encourage our coaches to inquire about school or to try and turn an article of clothing into a question. For example, if a boy shows up wearing a SpongeBob shirt, ask him who is favorite character is and why.

The coach asked this six-year-old wearing a purple Lord Jeff—Amherst College shirt, "Do you live in Amherst?" The six-year-old responded, "No, this is Amherst College." The coach answered, "Oh, you mean UMass–Amherst?" The six-year-old repeated, "No, I said Amherst College." The upshot of this exchange was that despite living twenty miles away from the second-ranked liberal arts college in America, this high school junior had no knowledge of it, and was aware of UMass being in Amherst only because of its nationally prominent basketball team. On the other hand, the six-year-old was quite savvy about Amherst College, UMass, and other colleges in the area.

The interchange reminded us of another episode in the early years of Project Coach. We had assembled our twenty teenage coaches for a workshop on the college application process. We asked an admissions officer to help us design an information session to help our teens think about the necessary steps. The first exercise was to identify somebody that they knew well whom they could interview about his or her experience of applying to, selecting, and attending college. After explaining the exercise, there was a long and uncomfortable silence that quickly devolved into off-task behavior. As things were unhinging, the question was asked, "How many of you know somebody who went or goes to college?" These young people came from Holyoke, a city only a few miles from four leading colleges, yet having a child poverty rate of nearly 40 percent.[19] *Only two of twenty youths were able to identify people in their social orbit who had attended college.*

One director described the mindset that the programs attempt to create: "These young people need to see college as inevitable. One of our jobs is to provide a myriad of experiences that surround youth with the idea that college is possible, inevitable, and just what you do after finishing high school. Middle class kids just know they will go to college." This mindset flowed through many of the programs we explored. The programs collectively serve to help young people think about who they might become in the future, their "possible selves." Possible selves encompass the beliefs about who one hopes or expects to become, as well as who one fears becoming.[20] The notion of possible selves is believed to influence a person's sense of self and motivation in two ways. First, it provides a clear and particular goal to strive toward or to avoid. Second, a clear view of self energizes an individual to self-regulate and take the actions necessary for moving toward their goal. As one young woman who was preparing to head off to college in the fall after a six-year-run with StreetSquash said,

> So many of my friends in school said they wanted to go to college, but they didn't do what they needed to do in school and otherwise. They made bad decisions, failed classes, and didn't stick to the plan. StreetSquash and all the tutoring, the counselors, the coaches, and everything they did for me kept me straight on track . . . They helped me see and believe that college could happen and they helped me every step of the way.

The idea of possible selves can exert a concrete impact on how one views oneself, plans, initiates actions, and negotiates adversity. These programs cultivate the notion of attending college as part of their community of practice and community ethos. Such aspirations are not just "pie in the sky" dreams, but reinforced by program activities, such as tutoring and school monitoring, and by the daily interactions participants have with staff who have graduated from an array of highly selective institutions.

GROWTH MINDSET: CONTENDING WITH ADVERSITY

When fourteen-year old Sharlene walked through the lunchroom in her Boston middle school, it was loud and raucous, the seventh and eighth graders chatting with each other, all the while jockeying for status amid the peer hierarchies and cliques. As she walked toward the door, she noticed a white woman in athletic clothes standing next to a strange-looking mechanical contraption. It looked like something gym-related, but Sharlene said, "I had no idea what it was." Sharlene's eyes lingered just enough for the woman to say, "Would you like to try?"

When we interviewed Sharlene she was a college senior, and when she told the story, she paused to compose herself. "Everything about the moment made me want to keep moving. I don't know why I stopped and answered her, but I did. I wonder what would have been if I didn't stop."

Sharlene grew up in the Boston communities of Dorchester and Roxbury. Her family—her mother, sister, and brother—was unable to pay the rent and had to move thirty-six times. She was accustomed to switching schools and passing through indifferent institutions, so she surprised herself when she stopped and let the woman show her how to sit down on the indoor rower, known as an ergometer, or by rowers as "the erg." The woman at the erg helped Sharlene, who was broad shouldered and athletic, take a few practice strokes. Nancy was on a recruiting mission for her organization, G-Row, which describes itself as a "rowing and relationship-building program designed specifically for girls in the Boston public schools." G-Row's mission is to "build girls' strength and confidence, and also aims to diversify the traditionally exclusive sport of rowing."

After a quick spin on the erg, Sharlene was intrigued, and she took some information and brought it home to her mother. She had never known about the sport, but as she became absorbed into the community of practice at G-Row, Sharlene started to practice three to four days per week. "I learned how to row, but also about training, swimming, boat repair, and how to train hard for something," she says. In a sport where rowers are predominately white and nearly 60 percent come from families earning over $100K a year, the seven miles from Roxbury to a scull sliding across the Charles River was a vast journey.

"I had no idea what I was doing, but I stuck with it. I improved with help from all the coaches and others in G-Row and that was really powerful for me." Sharlene's observation matches what G-Row calls their two fundamental beliefs: First, adolescent girls need to form healthy relationships and a sense of belonging in order to truly express and be themselves. Second, rowing for girls promotes self-confidence, determination, strength, and personal growth in a tangible and powerful way. G-Row emphasizes that the habits learned could translate to "life off the water." The program names those essential qualities as "dedication, perseverance, responsibility, trust, compromise, continuous learning, hard work, courage, balance, and teamwork."

Sharlene stuck with rowing through high school. By the time she graduated, she was ready to compete in college and when she enrolled at Smith, she joined the college team. Her journey from complete novice to college athlete highlights the development of the prevailing mindset of these programs. Sharlene explains, "I learned that if I stick with something I will get better at it. If you work hard and keep at it, you can get somewhere."

Sharlene's commentary on her sojourn from her middle school cafeteria to crewing competitive races on the picturesque Charles River embodies the core attributes of what Stanford psychologist Carol Dweck calls a "growth mindset." Dweck's work focuses on how self-beliefs influence and affect behavior and achievement.[21] Her research indicates that mindset has significant effects on behavior and performance, particularly in the face of challenging tasks. The central premise of her work involves differentiating between two mindsets. One she calls "fixed," which entails a belief that capabilities, such as intelligence, personality, athletic ability, and general human capacity, are relatively static and immutable. In contrast, a "growth mindset" connotes that such assets are adaptive and subject to change through cultivation. She believes that mindset can impact all areas of a person's life, from academic success to personal and professional accomplishments.

This critical dichotomy has major implications for what we are willing to do, how much effort we are willing to expend, and how we think and feel about competitive endeavors. Those with more of a "fixed mindset" tend to be more protective of their self and public personas in that they wish to maintain the illusion of superiority. For example, if such an individual wishes to cultivate the persona of someone perceived to have a high IQ, then she will be very risk averse to situations in which this identity might be challenged. Those who believe that ability and talents are fixed feel that they have a certain amount and nothing can be done to change it. Being overly concerned with manifesting talents and abilities, hiding deficiencies, and reacting defensively to mistakes or setbacks leads people to avoid seeking critical opportunities that would help them to learn and grow, since they typically do not wish to put themselves in positions that might challenge their personas. Clearly, such a brittle approach can severely limit one's willingness to stretch for new experiences.

On the other hand, programs such as G-Row are incubators of the "growth mindset." Here, the prevailing focus is on developing potential, promise, and possibility. Program leaders recruit young people not for their refined talent in crew, squash, art, or music, but for their willingness to commit to the process of learning how to grow. They seek young people who are willing to commit to a community of practice and to pursue personal and collective development by showing up, practicing, accepting critical feedback, and taking on challenges with indeterminate outcomes. In other words, getting good at the activity matters, but only if improvement is a by-product of the more fundamental process—cultivating a growth mindset.

We came to understand this difference in mindsets when talking to a coach who worked at G-Row, while simultaneously serving as a coach to a highly competitive elite team. Both programs are run out of the sleek 30,000-square-foot Harry Parker Boathouse on the Charles River. The competitive team unabashedly describes itself as "an unparalleled standard for youth development, winning more medals than any other program at US Youth Nationals and Canadian Henley." Youth rowers compete on teams that routinely send athletes to powerhouse national crew programs at Harvard, Yale, Princeton, Dartmouth, Penn, Syracuse, Washington, and Cal Berkeley.

Speaking to us amid the memorabilia of past races and pictures of old champions of the sport, Coach Brent Bode offered a thoughtful commentary on how these two types of programs function in the same physical space despite having distinctive philosophies and purposes. The competitive crew team spends the majority of its time on developing high-level performance through high-intensity training emphasizing technique. In contrast, the G-Row girls have a more comprehensive program that includes tutoring, mentoring, and academic advising in addition to rowing.

As Coach Bode wrote to us after our meeting, "Our CRI girls come from some of the most competitive environments in the U.S. If you remember from a *New York Times* article about some teens in Newton, MA, a few years back: 'For Girls, It's Be Yourself, and Be Perfect Too.'"[22] The article he refers to received much acclaim because it profiled a series of girls from the suburbs of Boston and described them as "amazing girls":

> Esther and Colby are two of the amazing girls at Newton North High School here in this affluent suburb just outside Boston. "Amazing girls" translation: Girls by the dozen who are high achieving, ambitious and confident (if not immune to the usual adolescent insecurities and meltdowns). Girls who do everything: Varsity sports. Student government. Theater. Community service. Girls who have grown up learning they can do anything a boy can do, which is anything they want to do.
>
> But being an amazing girl often doesn't feel like enough these days when you're competing with all the other amazing girls around the country who are applying to the same elite colleges that you have been encouraged to aspire to practically all your life.

As Coach Bode wrote to us:

> Many of the novice girls we have on our team are these highly motivated young people with big dreams and high expectations from wealthier, privileged households. It's no wonder that we have one of the fastest novice girls teams in the country because I don't need to do much in order to keep the girls on task. They want to be challenged from a very young age. Conversely, I'm usually reminding them to have more fun and to climb more trees, instead of studying more.

In other words, Coach Bode recognizes that the girls who crew the boats for the competitive rowing teams embody the most rarefied forms of concerted cultivation described by Lareau. One girl in the article describes this pressure:

> "You're supposed to have all these extracurriculars, to play sports and do theater," said 17-year-old Julie Mhlaba, who aspires to medical

school and juggles three Advanced Placement classes, gospel choir and a part-time job as a waitress. "You're supposed to do well in your classes and still have time to go out. You're supposed to do all these things and not go insane."

Sharlene rowed with these girls occasionally, but even their schedules did not mesh since the G-Row girls arrived right after school, after being picked up in a van by the coach, while the competitive rowers arrived much later—dropped off, he said, by a fleet of Volvos and high-end SUVs. These two programs share the same boathouse, the same river, the same coaches, and in some manner the same aspiration—to provide these young people an opportunity to succeed and thrive. However, the guiding framework and practices that organize the daily experiences of the two groups are different. To Coach Bode and his colleagues, the "amazing girls" emphasize a growth mindset to be successful rowers and move them toward their goal of higher rowing performance. G-Row emphasizes all of the same skills as well as mentoring, tutoring, enrollment in enrichment programs, and more. For these rowers, a growth mindset has less to do with being an elite rower and more with becoming a more resilient, capable, and adventuresome person.

All the programs we examined embraced this extra responsibility. Zack Lehman, the founder of MetroLacrosse, described how he first aspired to have his lacrosse players compete equally on the field with their age-mates from the suburbs in Brookline, Newton, and Wellesley. The idea of equal competition became complicated when he realized that the youth they worked with needed an array of academic supports. Lehman described how MetroLacrosse needed to cut back on practice time to focus on academic skills: "On the athletic front our kids weren't developing as fast as they would have athletically had we dropped them into Newton. But, for us, the compromise was worth it."

Sharlene confirmed this pattern: "As I advanced in crew, I got more deeply involved with G-Row and all the supports that helped me keep on moving forward." Another Smith student who played squash at Squash-Busters through high school said:

I didn't want to play squash when I came to Smith, I was ready to move on, but the lessons of working hard, getting help from others, and staying organized stayed with me. I mean I was a kid from Roxbury and I learned how to play squash. I wasn't really an athlete other than double-dutch, which I learned with my cousins, but I learned squash. I never got to be really good, but I got better little by little. When I got to Smith, I was way behind with my academics, but I learned how to make it in the same way—little by little.

Thus, when young people are in supportive environments, encouraged to experiment with novel activities, reinforced for expending effort, and shielded from the psychological bite of failure, their beliefs about achievement become more adaptable. They begin to understand the connection between working hard and attaining goals that at one time may have seemed impossible. Most importantly, when these youth move through adolescence, a time when beliefs about achievement and intelligence crystallize, and encounter new contexts where success and failure matter more and grades, rankings, high-stakes tests, and other structures shape their everyday experience, having a growth mindset can make all the difference in how they fare.

BUILDING RESILIENCE

In November 2008, the legendary General George W. Casey Jr., the army chief of staff and former commander of the multinational force in Iraq, had a conversation with Martin Seligman, the University of Pennsylvania psychologist often called the father of positive psychology. General Casey was concerned that the open-ended nature of the Iraq and Afghanistan wars had resulted in cumulative levels of stress among American soldiers, impacting their performance, their readiness, and—in many cases—their personal relationships.

The general and the psychologist followed up with each other and agreed to launch an unprecedented initiative that would strive to build positive assets and resilience skills within the army. The basis of the program was grounded in PERMA: positive emotion, engagement, relationships, meaning, and accomplishment—the building blocks of resilience and growth.

The most intensive element of the programming—master resilience training (MRT)— focused on building the "resilience muscle" in soldiers. To do this, they designed a sequence of workshops to build three distinct elements: mental toughness, signature strengths, and strong relationships.

A similar type of approach is often used by sports psychologists and others concerned with optimizing talent. They label it "mental skills training" (MST), which is designed to improve sport performance, enhance enjoyment, and help athletes develop life skills. A typical MST approach teaches an array of psychological skills that help focus attention, regulate thoughts, and manage emotions. The course of study used by coaches or consultants is linear and grounded in a three-step pedagogical approach. First, introduce the technique and provide opportunities to practice it under the guidance of a clinician. Second, practice the skill on one's own in a controlled environment. Last, after sufficient rehearsal, deploy the technique in "live" situations.

The programs that we observed attempt to produce outcomes similar to the aims of MRT and MST by cultivating norms and expectations within the various activities they run. For example, Artists for Humanity has a structure where artists move through a very explicit set of art tasks and experiment with a broad range of different art forms. In the process, the norms of revision, meeting deadlines, and professionalism get woven into the experience of producing art. In essence, MRT-like and MST-like knowledge and skill are conveyed as an organic part of what is learned within the community of practice on a daily basis. Indeed, the connection between normal program activities and developing such resilience skills is so tightly interwoven that staff sometimes seemed surprised by our questions probing whether these things were taught. After we explained what we meant, they typically smiled and conveyed, in one way or another, that the youth were learning these things from everything that they did as a participant in their programs.

Project Coach has taken somewhat of a hybrid position on teaching resilience skills. We have attempted to weave in explicit lessons to teach such things as goal setting, emotional regulation, attention control, and recovering from setbacks. In our travels, we learned that other programs also balance teaching these skills, both implicitly and explicitly. StreetSquash, for example, uses goal setting as a core strategy for teaching everything from striking a squash ball more effectively to improving one's algebra grades or managing emotions. Ultimately, however, connections among such skills are solidified by engaging in the practices associated with normal program activities.

As we were told by a StreetSquash staff member, if a youth has targeted emotional control in her goal-setting program, coaches are more effective in working on this in the midst of competition, when things are not going so well, than when sitting in a classroom using hypothetical examples. As Wenger contends, "Practice does not exist in the abstract. It exists because people are engaged in actions whose meaning they negotiate with one another."[23] Clearly, there are different pedagogical strategies for teaching the array of knowledge and skills that cultivate a resilient and positive mindset. For the most part, however, the organizations that we observed were more organic, flexible, and naturalistic in how they went about this. Through their more naturalistic pedagogy, they affirmed Wenger's contention that reflective engagement provides a powerful way to teach important life lessons.

In putting all of this together, we conclude that a large part of participating in the out-of-school programs that we observed is a complex combination of identity formation and ways of thinking about oneself and the world in which one lives. When an adolescent begins to think of himself as an artist, a squash player, a coach, or a prospective college student, he or she creates a persona that can be tried out, developed, and embraced in a safe and supportive environment. Irrespective of the specific core activity, all the programs have a common ethos of positive energy and upward mobility. Acquiring the sense that one will get better at the activity by working hard and being disciplined is the most obvious message from this engagement. The notion that the same formula works in school, or whatever else one does, is the real takeaway.

The scaffolding needed to make such lessons a reality is quite complex. It entails implicitly and explicitly teaching kids how successful people think. Having educational goals, a growth mindset, a sense that one has a voice in determining one's fate, and a positive outlook, even when faced with adversity, are elements of what programs aim to instill in participants. They also provide ample supports to reinforce these modes of thought, such as tutors and mentors. In most programs, grades are also monitored on a regular basis and connections made with teachers to make certain that participants are progressing satisfactorily. Additionally, an array of supercognitives is taught to provide youth with assets that will enhance performance and/or inoculate them against diversions that can impede achievement.

Whether the approach was explicit, implicit, or a hybrid, we observed emotional regulation, attentional control, conflict avoidance, self-awareness, perseverance, teamwork, and communication skills being taught and learned. That kids who stay with these programs, according to the program leaders we interviewed, graduate from high school and enter college at rates unprecedented for their demographic is testament to the powerful impact that these programs have on how participants think about themselves, their communities, and the world in which they live. In the next chapter we attempt to explain why we think youth stay with such programs—for years.

CHAPTER FIVE

Intrinsic Motivation
Energized from Within

I don't have to be here. But I am here all the time.
—SEVENTEEN-YEAR-OLD SQUASH PLAYER

E ven though activities such as squash and art can be engaging to youth, the truth is that American teenagers can be highly critical, fickle, and impulsive about how they apportion their time and attention. In our work with youth over the years, we were repeatedly struck by their consumer mentality toward school, our program, and all else in their life. If they perceived what was going on as boring, they tuned out. As youth culture critic Elissa Moses famously observed, *"Do not bore this generation or it will abandon you."*[1]

Given this mercurial developmental profile, programs face formidable challenges: How do you appeal to the fickle tastes of adolescents? How do you keep youth involved long enough to develop critical skills in an activity, and then begin to transfer what they learn to other domains in their life? How do you tempt youth, who could choose to spend their time in a near infinite array of activities, to spend many hours in a program? In truth, one of the most remarkable achievements of these programs may be finding ways to appeal to teenagers so that they willingly stay long enough, and engage with enough energy, to acquire the assets and the mindsets (as discussed in chapter 4) to change the trajectories of their lives.[2] As Greg Zaff, the executive director of SquashBusters, said, "If we have young people for enough time and for enough years, we can really make a difference. Keeping them in the program over the years is incredibly hard. I see this as the greatest challenge for our program and, to be honest, every program that does this work."

Each of the programs we learned about had different approaches to contending with this fundamental challenge. Everything from paying kids for their training and work, as is done in Project Coach, Artists for Humanity, and the Hyde Square Task Force, to offering national and international travel opportunities, as is done in StreetSquash, has been used to reward consistent, positive, and long-term participation. However, we believe that such extrinsic reinforcement plays only a part in whether youth embrace a program for years. In considering the wider range of reasons why kids join and stick with programs, we came to believe that the ideas of Edward Deci and Richard Ryan provide a useful framework for understanding this phenomenon.[3] As psychologists, Ryan and Deci explore what motivates people to find the energy to start a task and the discipline to persist at it. They distinguish between two approaches to motivation. The first they describe as driven by external factors—people engage in activities in exchange for various rewards such as money, status, or grades. The second approach entails motivation that derives from engaging in an activity. Here, participation itself becomes the reward as it satisfies a person's needs, interests, curiosity, and values. This has been labeled intrinsic motivation.

We believe that youth find that these programs satisfy their intrinsic needs. According to Ryan and Deci, these include fostering the development of competence in core activities, promoting deep and satisfying relationships among participants and staff, and sharing control over what is done, when it is done, and how it is done with the participants themselves. Competence entails having an effect on your environment and feeling like you are getting better at the activities in which you engage. As one young person told us when we asked her how her feelings about the program have changed over the years, she said, "As I became better and started to compete, I felt like I joined a family." The need for competence shapes our identity and sense of who we are. We often think about ourselves in relationship to the things we are good at (as in "I am an artist" or "I am a musician"). Relatedness is the desire to feel connected and to belong. It encompasses the core quality of a community of practice. You belong to a tribe, you care about others, others care about you, and you forge interpersonal bonds. The last basic need, autonomy, is about feeling in control over the activities you choose and how you participate. It means being able to make choices about important elements in your life, rather than having them dictated by others.

What makes this theory an important lens in understanding the programs we explored is that Ryan and Deci believe that an individual's motivational framework hinges on the social context. As Ryan explains in an interview:

> We basically postulate that all human beings, regardless of culture and developmental level, have some basic psychological needs, and these needs—for autonomy, for competence, for relatedness—can be easily frustrated as well as easily supported by social environments. If one is in an environment where one or more of these needs are thwarted or blocked from satisfaction, people show decrements in well-being and decrements in motivation. Theory looks at how social contexts—work, home, school environments—affect the motivation and wellness of people residing in them.[4]

We believe that when programs provide opportunities for meeting these innate needs, young people are more likely to stay on board and show up fully present and ready to be engaged, and by so doing reap the associated developmental rewards.

A SPACE TO BE INTRINSICALLY MOTIVATED

Kim Hien, born to a Vietnamese mother and an absent Chinese American father, was raised in inner-city Boston. Her mother spoke virtually no English and held a relatively low-paying job. Despite her own struggles integrating into the larger flow of American culture, Kim's mom held a deep, abiding value in the power of education for her children. As Kim wrote:

> I am a human product of an attentive and caring immigrant mother, who made sure I didn't miss school or forget about homework; committed teachers who sat down and taught me how to read; bilingual education that helped me balance my Vietnamese/Chinese and American identity; and communities that instilled in me the meaning of community work.

When Kim was fourteen she, like so many of Boston's youth, applied for acceptance to Boston's exam schools. The pressure of the selection test was debilitating because as Kim described it, "The story that we internalized was that if you didn't get into Boston Latin your life trajectory would be over." Against the odds, Kim was accepted into Boston Latin Academy—the storied lighthouse school that counts iconic Americans like Ben Franklin, Samuel Adams, and Ralph Waldo Emerson among its alums. But she described Boston Latin as cold and intensely competitive.

> I was incredibly thrilled to be accepted, but once I got there I was lost. I hated my time there and felt so disconnected from the curriculum, from my classmates, and the teachers. I was lost and lonely.
>
> I had always loved learning and knowledge, but I couldn't find myself or my story in any of what I was learning or how I was learning. I didn't have anybody to talk with about what I was going through; my mother didn't understand and my younger siblings were involved in their own education. I had made it, but I was really struggling and then I found A-VOYCE.

A-VOYCE stands for Asian Voices for Organized Youth for Community Empowerment. Its mission is "to bring high school students together to use their voices in affecting positive change in the community through the power of dialogue and storytelling." The program educates youth on community development, urban renewal, cultural identity, and how to use a variety of communication technologies to develop and share personal stories with others. For Kim, the community of practice that she experienced at A-VOYCE became the space where she felt "most alive" and "effective." As she describes it:

> I dreaded school and I could barely contribute and participate, but in A-VOYCE I felt valued and important. I loved the work of discovering stories, learning about my background, and then developing a narrative flow to share what I learned. I also met my mentor at A-VOYCE; she was a graduate from Amherst College and she helped me understand myself and connect the various parts of my life. The work of A-VOYCE meant something to me. I belonged there; I enjoyed my time there and it was there that I found myself.

Kim's journey of discovery is brought to high relief in a speech she gave at a dinner describing her work in A-VOYCE.

> When I started, I was only a sophomore in high school. I was only 15 years old at that time. I had no slight idea of Chinatown's history. I did not know much about nonprofit organizations and had a very vague idea of its importance. What is affordable housing? Who are the prominent Asian Americans? Who is Sam Yoon? Three years ago, I was just your ordinary teenager who was unaware of many things about a place I would soon call my own community.
>
> These past three years at A-VOYCE have helped open my eyes to many different things I have never seen in my life. I have never been so happy with a particular interest and passion, and my heart belongs to community work. As I was looking through the dictionary one day to find the word "voice," this particular definition summarizes the purpose I am here today.
>
> Voice is the right to express an opinion. I have learned how important "voice" is and how even though you may have a voice, that does not guarantee you will be able to display it. As I had the right

to speak in front of you of how important youth development is to me and also to future young leaders, I thought how important it is to me to one day pursue a political career to make social changes and to represent those who do not have the opportunity to project their own voices. Once again, this dream would not have been realized at such an early stage without my beloved program, which is the Asian Voices of Organized Youth for Community Empowerment.

A-VOYCE, like so many of the programs we studied, provides rich, complex, and meaningful challenges to the youth who participate. It also provides intensive support so that youth like Kim not only try highly challenging activities, but also experience success that, as she says, imprinted deeply on how she viewed herself and her future. She describes A-VOYCE as a place where her skills and capacity grew, an activity where she had creative choice and discretion, and an environment where she was part of relationships that guided her forward. Importantly, her drive to stay involved with A-VOYCE had little to do with external incentives or rewards. Instead, as Ryan and Deci emphasize, her commitment emanated from her own intrinsic motivations.

Anybody who has worked with youth or parented an adolescent understands that young people often resist, defy, or ignore efforts to pressure them to conform to external expectations. Schools and classrooms are filled with complicated schemes, systems, and accounting structures that attempt to ensure that adolescents behave, learn material, and adhere to the institution's rules and expectations. They often don't work, and sometimes bring about negative consequences that include disinterest, passivity, and overt resistance.

Precisely because programs are voluntary, young people can be empowered to reveal a different presence from what they show in other settings. Here's an illustration. We hosted a teacher from one of the schools that our coaches attended. The high school coaches were running practices for elementary-aged students and we were giving the teacher a tour of our program. At one point she stopped and watched one of the adolescent coaches from her class working with his team. He was fully engaged with the children, playing soccer tag and all the while keeping up a running commentary to the third graders. "Great move Raul! Johnny, you must have gotten faster last week, I can't catch you! Linda, nobody can ever figure that spin move!" His energy was vibrant. He exuded a playful, kid-friendly charisma. He was confident, competent, and professional.

The teacher stared at Hector and shook her head. "I can't believe Hector and the others." (By "the others," she meant the other students from her school.) "They look, feel, act, and behave so differently here. They drive teachers crazy in our school with their lack of energy and commitment. Here they are communicating, engaging, and focused. It's a side of them that I don't think I've ever glimpsed." We followed up and asked her why it was important to see students in this type of situation. Her answer relates back to the overarching premise of Ryan and Deci:

> When a kid shows up in my room and he is one of twenty-five and he doesn't communicate, or he appears disengaged and not interested, I think it's because he is disengaged and uncommunicative. I know it's wrong, but that is sometimes what I think. Then I see him in this context and I realize it's not who he or she is. They are not disengaged people, but the environment of school or my class shapes that behavior. It revolutionizes how you think about them.

This realization meshes with the undergirding principle of Ryan and Deci's work—motivation is not a fixed attribute. Instead, factors and conditions in the social context shape a young person's experience and the motivation for a particular activity. In this case, they exuded competence, were given the authority to be in control of their practice, and were socially engaged with their players. As Daniel Pink writes, "Deci and Ryan say we should focus our efforts on creating environments for our inner psychological needs to flourish."[5] This is just what these out-of-school programs appear to be doing by emphasizing opportunities for youth to experience a sweet spot of the human condition: intrinsic motivation. To do so, they had to construct opportunities for youth to experience the interlocking qualities of becoming competent, related, and in control of their activities.

COMPETENCE IS EARNED THROUGH PRACTICE

As young people grow in competence, they start to imagine their future differently. There is a reciprocal connection between getting good at something and dreaming of future possibilities because of one's emerging expertise. Nakkula and Toshalis describe this:

> Imagination may fuel the vehicle of creativity and learning, but skill building is required to move the vehicle in the intended direction. In other words, while imagination fuels our dreams, the requisite skills are needed to drive them home. Skills are the strengths and aptitudes we possess now. Skill development begins where we are and links our current, stable capacities with those that lie at the edge of our abilities. In this manner, skill development turns our potential into a tangible, personal possession or characteristic.[6]

The sense of getting better is a powerful motivating force for continuing to work hard. "I liked squash when I first started playing it, but I really enjoy it now that I am better at it," said one of the teens we interviewed at the Urban Squash National Tournament. These programs provide opportunities for young people to develop competence in a variety of domains. They also teach the processes by which they can become competent in whatever they choose to do. Whether the domain is art, squash, music, or school, the same formula can be applied. Competence requires appropriate learning experiences and hard work; it does not emerge spontaneously.[7] The structures, environment, setting, feedback, and relationships contribute toward the development of competence and the associated feelings of satisfaction that are experienced as competence grows. As one young person said in describing her time in a Boston youth program devoted to teaching dance to younger children, "I loved coming because I was getting better and it made me feel good to improve."

We heard similar sentiments on one of our visits to Artists for Humanity. We stopped to stare at a set of wildly painted chairs. They were student desk chairs, but painted with vibrant reds, deep blues, and brilliant yellows. Some were repetitive designs, some followed a theme, and others had free-flowing, seemingly random geometric shapes swirling to and fro. Susan Rodgerson watched us study the chairs. It was clear that she was taking pride in the talent of the youth in her program. She then turned and looked out across the gallery and said, "This works because our young people derive such satisfaction from creating something beautiful. We are here and we do what we do because we give young people a chance to find mastery."

We continued walking through the gallery with her and she stopped to look at a painting that a young Asian teenager had just begun. The sketch was a combination of pencil and color. The expression on the painter's face conveyed shyness, even retreat, yet there was also a boldness and a sense of confidence in her demeanor. Perhaps it was her concentration as she worked, wearing oversized headphones, that prevented her from noticing that we were observing her. The young artist moved confidently with her brush. Watching her, Rodgerson said,

> Our primary goal is that the young people that come into this program learn how to be self-sufficient. That they've figured out how to figure out the world. They know what their strengths are. They're courageous. They have enough of a base of knowledge where they can discover that discipline and practice equals results. And that happens in art making. You learn that, OK, if I focus on this, and practice this, I'm going to get somewhere.

As she spoke, she became animated, and several of the young people looked up from their colorful canvases. She looked at them and said, "Discipline plus practice—it gets results." They smiled and she smiled back. It was clearly a "mantra" that made sense to this diverse group of young people.

We kept on walking and Susan continued:

> Discipline plus practice. It's a process that is intentional. You know, most of these kids have never seen an artist's brush. Your first painting is pretty fundamental. Then kids are here three days a week,

three hours a day practicing. The next painting is better. The third painting it's like, "Wow, I didn't think I could do that!" That drives them to work harder. The direct result of witnessing their own development is one of the key factors for why kids focus, apply more discipline and get more results, and I think that's transferable, that's a life skill. And they have tangible, verifiable evidence in their face. They knew they couldn't paint well before and now they can.

Rodgerson's description of what happens in the studio matches what Csikszentmihalyi and Schneider found in their study of teenagers—teens derive enjoyment from productive activities.[8]

In all the programs that we examined, young people experienced the journey from starting as a raw novice to getting better at something. In this journey, they learned that it feels good to be competent, and they delighted in being able do the work. As one young artist said as we looked over his shoulder, "I love turning my ideas in my head into something that others can understand when they are on my paintings." A young artist from Hyde Park said, "I learned that I could help younger children make better decisions. I was good at that, and that matters to me." The experience of gaining skills and deploying them in the programs matters greatly. As Rodgerson said,

> We have this new group of older kids, who are drop-out kids and incarcerated youth, and they're up there saying, "I had no idea I could draw!" They're happy to do this, smiling from ear to ear; they've never done it before. They came here and they found out they were talented.

It would be misleading to perceive Rodgerson's story as some kind of magical moment, where a young person picks up a paintbrush and suddenly is drawing flowing landscapes. The spaces that called to the adolescents we spoke with were not magical. Rather, they had the feel of an active and busy workshop where mistakes happen, the process is messy, and learners fall all along the continuum. This kind of environment helps to alleviate what Elkind identifies as an adolescent's developmental phase marked by a heightened sense of self-consciousness, such that teens imagine that their behavior is the focus of everyone else's concern and attention.[9] Halpern describes how apprenticeships in such programs work to soften adolescent egocentrism: "It is not about them, not about their preoccupations. The focus is on the work at hand (rather than the adolescents per se). Performance is evaluated within the framework of standards that are part of an explicit, valued tradition."[10]

We heard about this when we visited Zumix. The building, Engine Company 40 Firehouse, abandoned for thirty years, is on the corner of Sumner and Orleans Streets in a largely immigrant neighborhood of East Boston. After a $4.6 million renovation funded entirely by Zumix, the space now has a beautiful performance studio, rehearsal rooms, and a state-of-the-art mixing workroom. As Kim Dawson, the program director, explained, they have a program that prepares participants to be audio engineers. As she talked, we looked at the booth, which contained numerous stations and hundreds of knobs, dials, and gadgets. It was unfathomably imposing in its complexity, but it was the authentic technology needed to manipulate sound levels and organize a sound recording. In describing what young people must do, Dawson said:

> We work with them to master these components. We expect them
> to be professional, and they are. It's a real recording studio and they
> learn to do the work, run the systems, take feedback, and work as a
> team. It's youth driven and self-directed, but they stay because they
> are committed to the work.

Acquiring the knowledge and skill to work this equipment is a significant achievement and produces the positive feelings of competence that sustain long-term involvement in the program.

Another support for building a sense of competence involves the material rewards that participants may acquire through their participation. Both Project Coach and Artists for Humanity pay adolescents for the work that they do. While pay often is perceived as an extrinsic reward it can also be interpreted by participants as evidence that they are valued for the competence that they bring to a program. One of the most poignant days we ever experienced in Project Coach had nothing to do with what happened on the field. We were three weeks into our fall programming and we had just finished running a soccer session for 125 or so elementary-aged players. (Each session ends with a debrief; then, once the actual sports session ends the coaches make a beeline to their bags and whip out their lifelines to the world. The freneticism of the phone grab resembles the level of activity after the New York–Boston morning shuttle lands at Logan and the pilot says, "You may now turn on your electronic devices.")

We were already walking to the car when Juanita came running over and said with desperation, "Somebody stole my phone, it's not here!" She then pulled out everything inside her backpack and shook it on the ground. She was teary, but not from sadness. She was fuming mad. "I just bought this phone. It is my first phone and I bought it with my own money. It's my first paycheck! I can't believe this." And then she started to cry. "I bought this with my own money. I finally had a phone that I liked."

Juanita's phone was stolen from her bag that day. We never recovered it and Project Coach ultimately bought her a replacement. Her fury and sadness reminded us that this was the first "real" employment held by the teens in our program. She was devastated because she had bought the phone with money that she had earned from her very own paycheck. Juanita lived with different families and cousins. She slept on a couch in a room with a number of other teenagers and younger children. While the mission of Project Coach appealed to her and the idea of serving as a leader was motivating, the paycheck, the job, and the self-worth that comes from feeling valued and becoming self-sufficient were powerful forces running through her experience in our program.

The role of paid employment in youth programs is not insignificant. Jobs for youth are sparse. The consequences of low teen and young adult employment rates are far reaching. Work is where many teens "find themselves" because they can shine in ways that go unrecognized in schools preoccupied with the acquisition of decontextualized knowledge. Research also shows that the more individuals work during their teen years, the more they work and earn as adults: "Work experience in the teen years is a valuable form of human capital investment. Teens need more of it."[11] Work environments can be crucial settings to develop the "soft skills" needed to compete and succeed in the workplace.

Importantly, most programs do not routinely employ youth as part of their theory of change and operating framework. Three notable exceptions are Artists for Humanity, Project Coach, and the Hyde Square Task Force. All three ascribe to the belief that paying youth recognizes their commitment, skill, and unique capacity to contribute. Paid employment not only serves as extrinsic motivation, but also provides participants with a sense of competence, accomplishment, and tangible recognition of their capacity and contribution. In essence, it makes youth feel valued for their ability to deliver a service. As one of the youth we interviewed at Hyde Square said, "The work was with the community and for the community, but it was also for me. I loved the job and earning money. I didn't ever have to ask my mother for clothes money. I bought it on my own. I also paid for my own cell phone. It made me feel independent."

The paid element of these programs can and should be seen as providing both competence and autonomy, two of the major factors in Ryan and Deci's model of intrinsic motivation and self-determination.

RELATEDNESS AND COLLABORATION

The research on intrinsic motivational processes describes how genuine enjoyment takes root in contexts where people feel a sense of connectedness and belonging. In contrast, when people feel relationally insecure or alienated, they are more inhibited and defensive and less likely to experience interest or enjoyment in their activities. In other words, feeling rejected, isolated, and unappreciated tends to undermine intrinsic motivation.

One of the remarkable features of these programs is the shoulder-to-shoulder work done by youth and adults together. For example, on Summer Sunday in Piers Park, Zumix youth work alongside adult staff coordinating the events, handling the logistics, and setting up the stage, lighting, and sound systems. On Wednesday afternoons in Project Coach, teenagers huddle up with veteran Springfield teachers doing their last bits of preparation before the kids arrive. The teachers and teenagers will co-teach a literacy and writing lesson using a children's book about Roberto Clemente. Sitting around a table in Artists for Humanity, a group of four teenagers and two adults is talking about a sculpture design for a client. The ideas whip back and forth and the discussion sounds like that of a highly proficient creative team.

These brief examples convey a differentiating attribute of these programs: they all entail a depth and intensity of collaborative practice between adults and youth. What makes this form of collaboration distinctive and developmentally important to youth is its purposeful nature. Both youth and adults work jointly toward the production of a tangible product or service.

Lissa Soep, an irrepressible dynamo who has long worked in the area of youth and adults co-creating has written and talked about this special quality of relatedness as "collegial pedagogy." In a presentation she did for our class on youth development, she described her work as research director and senior producer at Youth Radio, a youth development organization and independent media production company founded in Oakland, California, in 1992. Youth spend afternoons in the Oakland facility developing stories, writing, and shaping their commentaries and reports into content that will be delivered on deadline to commercial, public, and community-supported radio stations, including National Public Radio. After sharing the mission of the organization, which is "to promote young people's intellectual, creative and professional growth through training and access to media and to produce the highest quality original media for local and national outlets," Soep described the collegial approach that unfolds between adults and youth in the studio:

> As adults, we work alongside teenagers shaping and crafting the programs, and questions of quality are crucial. This focuses our attention on working together in ways that create a special relationship.

We co-create in ways that enable us to pull off work that we could not do alone. Not only do we need each other to craft the work, but we send it off to an audience that judges the work in ways that we can't control.

For Soep, the entwinement of youth and adults working together on an authentic, high-stakes, public product drives a form of constructive relationship that is rare for young people *and* adults to experience. In a book focused on the work of Youth Radio, Soep and her coauthor Vivian Chavez elaborate on this co-creative process:

> In collegial pedagogy, emerging and established producers jointly create original work for public release, engaging a process that has significant potential to deepen the learning experience for both parties . . . Collegial pedagogy also raises serious challenges for young people and adults. It entails collaboration across differences in power as it manifests through age, position, and experience, and sometimes race, class, and gender. Relentless deadlines and mutual creative investment intensify the undertaking for all involved.[12]

The forms of relatedness that grow from the joint production of high-stakes projects involve immediacy and shared respect. The mutuality and reciprocity that emerge when working together reframe relationships in ways that young people find powerful. In Soep and Chavez's work, they describe a production cycle around a story about sex education and sexual values held by teenagers. The story idea came from National Public Radio, which was preparing a broadcast about a national poll on sex education and abstinence, and producers wanted a companion story in the voice and perspective of youth. Soep and Chavez describe how a story moves through the editorial stage to the creative framing of the piece (including an engaged discussion on how to appropriately frame the story for a larger audience), to production that results in an air-ready product. Woven through the entire cycle is an emphasis on the "mutuality of joint production." It is a way of being with youth that is not contrived and metaphoric, but grounded in producing something authentic.

> They literally co-create a media project through an intricate cocompositional process shot through with opportunities and risks . . . young people and adults actually make work together, revealing their investments and vulnerabilities to one another in concrete ways.[13]

It is, as Soep and Chavez conclude, a "hand-in-hand" process.

Another version of the collegial pedagogy is illustrated during a dismissal at Project Coach. A grandfather who speaks little English shows up to pick up his fourth-grade granddaughter. The girl lives with her grandparents, as the parents are no longer in the neighborhood. Like many of our participants of both genders, she is showing signs of obesity. The grandfather comes up to one of our graduate student supervisors and tries to start a conversation. The student, who graduated from a highly competitive college but speaks no Spanish, starts looking around anxiously for help. He calls to an adolescent coach named Talana who comes over and easily and comfortably greets the grandfather in Spanish. Talana translates the conversation that ensues. The grandfather is concerned about his granddaughter's weight because of what the doctor had said about the risk of type 2 diabetes. With Talana leading the conversation, the three talk about exercise and diet. The grandfather warmly shakes Talana's hand and nods to the graduate student. The student then turns to Talana and says, "You are so brilliant. That was such an important conversation for that grandfather, and I could have never had it without you." Talana smiles and during our debrief, describes how important and useful she felt as part of the "team" that helped this girl and her family. Such reciprocal and mutual relationships are especially powerful and meaningful.

AUTONOMY

At the core of Ryan and Deci's theory of motivation is the concept of control. If our goal is to create environments in which children are self-motivated, then we must make certain that they feel they are being taken seriously, are respected, and have some control over what transpires in their daily lives. Youth who participate in activities controlled, choreographed, and scrutinized by adults are less likely to be motivated to engage in particular tasks. If anything, their main motivation may be to avoid or oppose the desires of others; a power struggle, uncooperative behavior, and anger are likely to ensue.

Briana Morales is a sixteen-year-old who lives with her mother and three siblings. She has never known her father. When she joined Project Coach she wanted a job and stated, "I wanted to give back to my community." She has an easy smile with the children she coaches and because she listens attentively during group discussions and workshops, has become a favorite among the staff and her peers. In late November, the program collects copies of the coaches' first-quarter report cards. When a staff member sits down with Briana, she can barely look him in the eye. Her voice is near a whisper and her eyes have the moist, blurry look that teens get when they are on the verge of raw emotion, but are working to hold it back. "I can't believe it. I did horrible. I had no idea. I failed almost everything," she says. "What were the grades?" the staff member asks. D in math, C– in English, F in history, and D in science. There is a long pause. Briana is trying to tap back her emotion, which comes through as sadness, frustration, and embarrassment. She clearly feels ashamed. "I have to do better," she says quietly, although with a grim tone. "I have to do better."

The prior week, Briana had been part of a focus group that was discussing whether Project Coach should hold teen coaches accountable for their grades. The discussion evolved out of a "case study" scenario that the coaches were deliberating about with staff. The case study focused on two youth sport coaches and the rules that they had developed for their teams. The first coach demanded respect, commitment, and hard work during practices and games. He was clear that what happened during school time and in their community interactions were important, but he could not hold them accountable for the decisions they made outside of his program. The second coach also ran a youth basketball program, but he was fully dedicated to holding young people accountable across the domains of their life. He demanded that players submit grades to him and he asked for teacher reports verifying that his players were behaving and performing with effort in their school responsibilities.

The question posed to Briana's group invited them to apply the lessons of the case study to Project Coach: "Should we continue to monitor your academics? Should participation in the program hinge on reports we get from your teachers and your grades?"

Briana was extraordinarily clear in her response. "I think that you should keep on checking up on us. If you don't, nobody does. My mother rarely asks me about grades and it feels good to be asked. I like that you check up on us." Briana's grades were so low she was now on official probation; however, as a staff member said to us:

> We would never release or cut Briana, but the dilemma that we have with her is the same that we have with so many of our kids. She is smart, engaging, and a person of huge promise, but how can we help her be more successful? How can we help her achieve?

Autonomy does not mean total freedom from acceptable behavioral standards. It also does not mean going solo. But it does imply having a say in one's own forward trajectory. So many of the young people we talked with spent time in schools and organizations that were structured around principles of command and control that did not incorporate their views. In an environment where oversight depends on compliance, young people feel discounted and diminished.

The emphasis at out-of-school programs, because they are voluntary, underscores principles of self-management. Participants do not want to be told what to do by others without having any input on what those things are. Instead, they yearn for the autonomy to express their individuality and make decisions about their own life and development. In the end, Briana was quite willing to develop a strategy to improve her school performance and to work closely with tutors that Project Coach made available to her. As Ryan and Deci have hypothesized, shifting control to participants can have a powerful impact on sustaining behavior without having to invoke extrinsic mechanisms. All the programs we learned about developed an ethos and systems that enabled youth to exercise autonomy and have an active and meaningful role in shaping the practices of the community. These programs were "loud with youth voice."

LOUD WITH YOUTH VOICE

Perhaps no more important decision for a programs is who is hired as staff. While programs differ in how they involve participants in this process, we have come to believe that it is critical in promoting the element of control that adolescents hold so dear. Project Coach now regularly involves its youth in selecting their prospective supervisors. The following anecdote provides a window into how these interviews go.

The lead interviewer smiled warmly and introduced himself. "Hi, I'm James." A second interviewer chimed in a little more assertively—perhaps channeling a little Donald Trump in *The Apprentice*—"Why should we hire you?"

The applicant, a recently graduated college athlete, paused, visibly grimaced, and nodded in the way people do when they are trying to gather their thoughts and poise. After a short bit, he resumed eye contact and said, "I think I have a lot to learn from you."

The panel members looked up and collectively smiled. It was an evocative moment to watch because the dynamics were complex. On one side of the table was a young man who, by most measures, embodied the resume of a rising star. He was a graduate of a college ranked "most competitive" in all the college guidebooks and possessed an athletic record of glowing accomplishments. On the other side of the table was a group of high school students from Project Coach.

The interviewers looked at each other as his response pulled them off the script of questions they had developed in advance of the interviews. They looked at each other, and then one of the adolescent panelists chimed in with a follow-up prompt they had discussed during the planning session: "Can you say more?"

The applicant nodded. "I have read about your program and I have heard about it, and I think that you know your program, your community, and your approach. I hope to learn from it."

The interviewers smiled as the applicant continued to describe how he hoped to learn about how programs like Project Coach can work with schools to support young people and the larger community. As he talked, they continued to smile and nod in affirmation of the applicant's ideas. The exchange continued and the interviewers proceeded through their protocol. At the conclusion of the session, the applicant stood up and shook hands again with each of the four teenagers who served on the panel. Luis told him, "It was nice to meet you and we will be back in touch after we discuss this with the rest of the team."

The interview panel sat back down and each member picked up a pencil and began to write about their impressions of the candidate. They did so emboldened and confident with the knowledge that they would get to share their views of the strengths and challenges of each applicant they interviewed. In short, the youth in Project Coach were integral participants in a process described to them as the most fundamental variable in Project Coach's success: hiring the right people.

Luis's firm handshake, eye contact, and confident response to the candidate represented an important facet of programs like Project Coach. He and his peers confidently and professionally participated in a decision that will impact their lives, their peers' lives, and their community. A growing body of research points out that youth yearn for and thrive when they have the ability to exert influence and power over the circumstances of their own lives and those around them.[14] The research calls this "agency" or "youth voice." Within these programs, young people are given a voice, asked for their input on an array of activities, and given selective decision-making power; they begin to learn how members of a community can gain control over their own lives.

One of the young people we spoke with described it simply: "I like making decisions that change things. I like being in the mix." She articulated what sociologists and psychologists describe as a paradigmatic principle of human development, which involves how important it is to have the ability to exert influence on one's life or the lives of others.[15] Participating in programs that provide young people with authentic opportunities to weigh in and collaborate with adults on resolving the inevitable questions about who, what, where, when, and how can help youth develop a sense of confidence, competence, and self-worth.[16]

Promoting and nurturing youths' voice plays an important part in engaging them, especially older high school students, who typically avoid out-of-school programs that do not give them a say in decision making or planning.[17] For many youth, the ability to influence the programs they participate in contrasts with the sense of powerlessness they feel in other contexts of their lives.[18] Because youth are often marginalized, they may opt to either disengage or rebel by rejecting institutional norms. Such lack of control over one's life is a precursor to "learned helplessness," and in the case of adolescents can contribute to diminished self-concepts, disengaging from school, cutting classes, underperforming academically, and even dropping out.[19] Michelle Fine describes this diminished form of personal power as being "silenced" where one carries on with "a terror of words, a fear of talk."[20]

In contrast, the prevailing ethos and practices of the programs we studied include young people in the crafting and deployment of the community processes. These programs seek to be spaces "loud" with youth voices. The mindset they cultivate—"I matter and I can say my piece and shape the context that I inhabit"—has powerful personal, social, educational, and political possibility.

While building internal assets such as an achievement-oriented mindset and intrinsic motivation are critical, building external resources to help young people access opportunities and overcome obstacles is also essential for promoting their development. In chapter 6 we turn to how programs can be vast resources for helping youth build their social capital.

CHAPTER SIX

Acquiring Social Capital

New Connections, New Contexts

The first squash court in the United States was reputedly built at St. Paul's School in New Hampshire. Founded in 1856, the prep school is set on two thousand acres of woodlands, lakes, and fields. It is considered an elite prep school and counts among its alumni J. P. Morgan Jr., Cornelius Vanderbilt III, John Jacob Astor IV, John Kerry, and many other sons and daughters of the American elite. From such a start, squash in the United States has a long tradition of being associated with other top-tier prep schools such as Exeter, Andover, and Choate, along with Ivy League schools such as Harvard, Yale, and Princeton, and highly selective East Coast colleges such as Williams, Amherst, and Wesleyan. In fact, in a marketing study commissioned by the U.S. Squash Association in an attempt to secure sponsors, the organization describes the sport as one of "unparalleled demographics." The following data give a snapshot of squash players in the United States:

- $287,000 is the average household income.
- $1,407,000 is the average family net worth.
- 98% have college degrees; 57% have graduate degrees.
- Squash players reside in 3 of the top 5, and 5 of the top 11, most frequent zip codes listed among the top 100 wealthiest zip codes.

These data are significant when one considers the potential of an activity to bridge socioeconomic classes. Clearly, diverse groups of people are not mingling in exclusive country clubs or in underresourced and underserved urban neighborhoods to play squash. However, when David Letterman, who is an avid squash player, could not reserve a court at the Downtown Athletic Club by Wall Street, he went to New York's newest squash facility, StreetSquash. The squash facility cost $9 million to build and it boasts, according to some squash aficionados, the poshest courts in Manhattan. Yet it is located in the Kalahari apartment building in historic Harlem on West 116th Street, where the average family income is about $22,000.

George Polsky conceived of and designed StreetSquash as a facility with a bricks-and-mortar academic center at its heart, with two classrooms and a library. Not only do the StreetSquash youth receive academic tutoring, but they also get connected with high-flying mentors from the financial district, corporate America, "rarefied" professionals, and a plethora of recent college graduates who attended many of the most selective colleges in the country. With real estate costing nearly $200 a square foot in central Harlem, this sports/academic initiative involves a formidable commitment.

StreetSquash's rich, plentiful, and multidimensional resources represent an intentional effort to advance the opportunities for young people who participate in their program. StreetSquash actively builds social and cultural capital, which can be understood as nonmonetary, community, and extended-community resources that confer advantages on children and usually correlate—albeit imperfectly—as a proxy for social class. Implied in the intensive investment of StreetSquash and other such programs is the theory that by infusing the lives of children with opportunities to cross social class lines, they will acquire the same sorts of assets that their more advantaged peers enjoy. In essence, they believe these bridging contacts and experiences can serve as a surrogate for the exposure to activities, experiences, and people that middle- and upper-class kids get simply by growing up in their concertedly cultivated worlds.

Squash, crew, art, music, and other such activities also support what admissions officers call a "special talent" or "hook" that provides a substantive, and perhaps crucial, boost in the "sharp-elbows" world of college admissions. For example, in 2007 the *New York Times* ran a story that caught fire on the blogosphere and on websites like College Confidential that are devoted to demystifying the nuances of the college admissions process. This article, titled "And for Sports, Kid, Put Down 'Squash,'" was nonapologetically and almost snarkily aimed at parents and youth who calculatedly think about how to acquire and deploy social and cultural capital:

> You've already enrolled your teenagers in advanced-placement Mandarin, retained a $9,000-a-year college admissions consultant to help refine their applications, and sent them off to Kyrgyzstan to dig irrigation ditches for the summer. Still, there's no guarantee that they'll get into an Ivy League university. What are you going to do? Like a small but growing number of parents, you might hand the kids squash rackets.[1]

WHAT IS SOCIAL CAPITAL?

Squash is a useful access point for this chapter, which focuses on how participation in the structured programs that we observed provides an infusion of social capital in the lives of underserved youth. An access point is a special path, an alternative to the "front door." Social capital also entails the relationships and experiences that provide resources and benefits to youth who are striving to get ahead—despite growing up without the connections and relationships that so often provide an advantage.

The founders, staff, funders, and others associated with the programs we examined conveyed a desire to connect the young people in their programs to the powerful social networks that had helped them to succeed. Zack Lehman, the charismatic founder of MetroLacrosse and himself a product of Philips Exeter, Dartmouth, and Harvard Law School, described in a phone interview how the founding of MetroLacrosse represented an intentional effort to counter the patterns of advantage:

> When my wife and I moved into Charlestown I was wearing my Dartmouth lacrosse jacket. A local cop saw me with the jacket and

asked if I played for Dartmouth. Over the next few months, I saw him a few times and he kept on asking if I would consider starting a lacrosse program for the kids in Charlestown, a community contiguous to Boston that has more public housing per square foot than any community in Massachusetts.

Lehman's impetus for launching MetroLacrosse operated on multiple levels. He wanted to share his passion and love for the sport of lacrosse with young people. He believed that the game of lacrosse has lessons to teach young people about discipline and confidence that can help them resist drugs and gangs. Just as important, he believed that getting kids involved in lacrosse, a sport that has thrived in affluent communities and in top-tier prep schools and colleges, could result in unanticipated positive outcomes for them. As his program grew, Lehman needed more volunteers to run clinics, coach teams, and serve as mentors to the players:

> The lacrosse community is really close and filled with genuine people. Pretty soon we had an influx of lacrosse players—they were mostly yuppies—and they were commuting from the Back Bay [an affluent Boston neighborhood] and teaching lacrosse and getting involved in these kids' lives. Kids were learning things about success and their future—mostly by just being around these successful lacrosse players.

The essential idea of social capital reads like a list of old saws from mom, dad, and the career development center: "build your network," "don't burn bridges," "cultivate mentors," and "join groups that can help you get ahead." In his important book *Bowling Alone: The Collapse and Revival of American Community*, the eminent Harvard political scientist Robert Putnam offers a straightforward conceptual definition:

> The core idea of social capital theory is that social networks have value. Just as a screwdriver (physical capital) or a college education (human capital) can increase productivity (both individual and col-

lective), so too can social contacts affect the productivity of individuals and groups.[2]

Social capital is not a "thing" or an "artifact"; it is a set of resources that inhere in relationships of trust and cooperation between people.[3] Social networks and capital have value. Individuals who cultivate relationships, build networks, acquire mentors, enlist allies, and form connections are building important resources to advance their interests in both the short and long term. The old axiom "it's not what you know, but who you know" has been empirically proven, as Putnam tells us: "Executives with bounteous Rolodex files enjoy faster career advancement."[4]

As a collective asset, social capital plays an important role in ensuring those aspects of growth, welfare, and development that an individual can rarely provide alone. For example, Putnam describes how

a well-connected individual in a poorly connected society is not as productive as a well-connected individual in a well-connected society. And even a poorly connected individual may derive some of the spillover benefits from living in a well-connected community. If the crime rate in my neighborhood is lowered by neighbors keeping an eye on one another's homes, I benefit even if I personally spend most of my time on the road and never even nod to another resident on my street.[5]

Social capital, thus, implies that dense networks of social interaction can facilitate cooperation and produce an array of benefits. As Putnam notes, it's a form of the Golden Rule: "I'll do this for you without expecting anything specific back from you, in the confident expectation that someone else will do something for me down the road."[6]

The general principle of social capital implies that humans are stronger, both individually and collectively, when bound together in networks. The research identifies two distinctive forms of social capital: bonding and bridging. Bonding social capital involves strong, durable relationships among the members of a group of people—a family, an affinity group, ethnic group, club, or religious organization. It constitutes what Putnam calls a "kind of sociological superglue."[7] These local communities depend on a high degree of fraternity and solidarity within the group. People depend on these affiliations for assistance when they face problems and challenges. Some sociologists discuss these types of social relationships as survival oriented in that they help poor and vulnerable individuals cope by providing stopgap support.[8] The various programs to which we allude and characterize as communities of practice tend to foster and possess a high degree of this sort of social bonding among their participants.

Bridging social capital represents ties and relationships to people who are unlike each other—who are of a different class, ethnicity, race, or generation. It implies reaching out and connecting beyond the boundaries of one's primary identity and a widening of what some scholars call the "social spiral," an idea derived from Alexis de Tocqueville, who argued that when individuals join a civic community, the meanings they develop through their interactions encourage a spiral outward.[9] As engagement among groups occurs, different meanings and ties are formulated and, most importantly, horizons are stretched.[10]

In sum, social capital is a resource that leads to productive networks that are guided by consensual norms and trusting relationships. Putnam calls social capital WD-40 because it lubricates social, civic, and economic life. When individuals interact regularly and trust one another, social transactions are more efficient and communal problems are more easily resolved.

SOCIAL CAPITAL IS IMPACTED BY CONTEXT

Yet, "soft relational" forms should never be viewed as a viable antidote to poverty and institutional neglect characterized by dysfunctional schools, poor health services, and systemic poverty. Warren, Thompson, and Saegert make this point in an introductory chapter to *Social Capital and Poor Communities*.[11] They remind readers who might be captivated by social capital as a panacea for endemic poverty that social capital is not an alternative to providing better jobs, schools, and public services to poor communities. They also clearly remind their readers that the causes of generational poverty cannot be attributed to tattered social capital processes. Poverty derives from broader economic, political, and racial structures of society. Poor inner-city neighborhoods, according to the research of William Julius Wilson, have suffered increasing rates of social dislocation and isolation—the antithesis of social capital—because the exodus of jobs and the flight of the middle class have created pockets of persistent intergenerational poverty.[12]

Conversely, affluent communities with greater financial resources and stronger institutions like school can derive more enduring benefits from social capital. For example, residents in a poor urban community may belong to the same church as or be friends with their neighbors, but those neighbors can't plug them into a network to land a high-paying job. Warren et al. offer a cogent illustration of how in poor communities even well-meaning and coalesced groups that may have systems of trusting interaction in place operate under a decided disadvantage. In an affluent community PTA, members come together and advance an agenda that promotes using the latest curriculum innovations and pedagogies. In contrast, PTA members in an inner-city school similarly come together, but instead of mounting a campaign to influence the character of classroom teaching, they devote their collective effort to devising a strategy to get a dysfunctional central bureaucracy to fix a deteriorating auditorium ceiling. The larger point is that bonding social capital is limited in combating the issues related to poverty. Warren et al. write, "Poor communities cannot solve their problems on their own, no matter how strong and well organized their internal social capital becomes. They require greater financial resources and better public services. Their residents need better education and human development."[13] To access such resources, bridging social capital is needed.

URGENT INTERVENTIONS: MOMENTS OF INFLUENCE

When we met staff and young people in programs, we were often introduced as professors from Smith College. Invariably, one of the staff members would say, "We have a young person who would be great at Smith."

Occasionally, the staffer would call over a young person and we would chat with them about their college plans or the offerings at Smith. This type of interaction typically involved social capital building. The following event is an example of what we view as "urgent intervention." In early May we received an e-mail from a staff member at one of the organizations:

> Jen mentioned that your colleague will be visiting soon and it got us thinking. We have a young woman who had to turn down Villanova because they didn't offer her enough financial aid and accepted Oneonta's offer [a state college in New York], which was heartbreaking for her. However, Smith just took her off the waitlist and she's in, which is hugely exciting for her. I was mentioning this situation to Susan and she mentioned that I should get in touch with you guys on the off chance you know someone and could advocate for her. As of last week, she had not received a financial aid award letter from Smith, and we worry that she'll be in the same situation as she was with Villanova. Do you guys know anyone or have any insight?

We trusted and admired the staff person, plus we were happy to provide some type of reciprocal response to an organization that had hosted us for multiple days and many interviews. We let the staff member know that we were on the case. She responded by saying,

> Hi, This is fantastic! Thank you for being so on our side!!
>
> Her name is Laura Jones, and she is amazing! She has all A's and B's in all AP courses, and is about to graduate from [one of the city schools]. She's first generation college going. She's studying Arabic and is so focused and a total superstar around here in her work, leadership, and work ethic. All the money she earns goes to her family and her college savings.
>
> Thanks for looking into it!

We contacted the admissions office, described the mission of the out-of-school program, and shared the e-mail. In response to our reaching out, an admissions officer contacted the staff member, and in the end, Laura ended up enrolled at Smith. The other longer-term outcome of this bridging event is that the Smith Admissions Office now has the program on its radar and will begin recruiting there in subsequent years.

The eventual conclusion to this story is still an open question. What we do know is that this intervention supported Laura's future at a critical juncture. Program staff who were knowledgeable about schools as well as Laura's capabilities and aspirations believed that Smith would be a good fit for her. Consequently, Laura's bridging social capital was leveraged, and she wound up with two advocates who were directly connected to people who could make enrollment at Smith happen.

Another example of a just-in-time social capital bridging occurred in Project Coach when James, one of our teens, was getting ready to start college. He would be the first in his family to attend college and his parents, who are both immigrants, divorced, and with no experience with higher education, were stumped about how to help their son. He received notice from the college that his FAFSA form had not been processed. It was mid-August and college loomed. He said: "When I first heard that my financial aid was missing, I panicked and thought there is no way I can go to college. I didn't know what to do and then I e-mailed my Project Coach mentor." Within hours program staff had called his college and touched base with the admissions office and financial aid staff. They also set up a time to meet him and his mother to help them refile the FAFSA form. A program staff member who headed up the effort stated:

> I remember how daunting these forms were in my own student days and I remember how my parents took care of almost everything. I can barely remember if I had any role in filling these out. When James e-mailed I felt the desperation. Nobody can afford college without financial aid and so I saw my role as supporting him by doing whatever needed to be done to get this situation fixed.

A third instance of how powerful social bridging can be is provided by Trevis, a seventh grader who participates in the Twin Cities Beyond

Walls Squash Program. Trevis, who attends a KIPP Academy in Minneapolis, conveyed to the squash program director that his family, consisting of his mother and three siblings, had just been evicted from their apartment and were now living in a shelter. We also learned that his mother's yearly income was approximately $2,000. Despite his family situation, Trevis is an honor student, and in sitting down and talking with him, one would be amazed at his maturity and thorough understanding of the various character traits taught by KIPP and Beyond Walls. Ask him what *empathy* means or what *grit* is and he can not only provide a definition, but give you examples of how they apply to his daily life. After such exchanges, one is somewhat taken aback by how such a young kid could be so thoughtful and engaging. In any event, through Beyond Walls Trevis learned about a five-week summer program at Philips Exeter Academy in New Hampshire that he really wanted to attend. This program contains a mixture of academic enrichment, sports, and local travel. Moreover, at least for five weeks, it would give him a respite from a difficult home situation, provide a pleasant place to live, and offer opportunities for enhanced learning. But the problem for Trevis was how to get from a homeless shelter to Philips Exeter, where the summer tuition was $7,900. As it turns out, the director of Beyond Walls learned that Philips Exeter, in conjunction with the National Urban Squash and Education Association, awards ten scholarships to the program, and all that Beyond Walls needed to do was come up with $2,000 to pay for such things as books and travel to and from New Hampshire. So, Trevis's name was put forward as a scholarship candidate. As his story permeated throughout the national network of people associated with the urban squash movement, several donors came forward and committed to supporting Trevis, whether he was one of the lucky kids to receive a scholarship or not. The bottom line is that Trevis was able to attend Philips Exeter for the summer because of the vast web of social capital that could be leveraged from Beyond Wall and its connection to a wider national network.

As Putnam describes it, social capital "greases the wheels." It serves as a timely "infusion" of influence needed to get ahead or to help negotiate a problem. For young people like Laura and James, the college admissions process looms as a mysterious phalanx. Not only do children of college graduates typically have more resources, both in understanding the proccss and having access to money, but they also often attend schools that have highly structured systems for assisting them throughout the college admissions process. The intricacies of college rankings, financial aid, wait lists, and other elements of the process often disadvantage poor and first-generation students. These urgent situations require mobilizing resources, making connections, and reaching out quickly. They also clearly fit the parameters of "moments of influence." For kids like Trevis, getting to the point where applying to college is even a possibility is fraught with all sorts of obstacles that can be devastating. Yet by joining programs and leveraging the social capital of their networks, staying on track becomes possible.

PIVOTAL ALLIES

In addition to providing social capital, these programs are also becoming institutions that represent and promote the interests of their participants. With founders and staff who are often connected with institutions of power and prestige, they are increasingly recognized as the "go to" organizations for colleges that wish to recruit a more diverse student population. Urban out-of-school organizations have cachet with some of the best colleges and universities in the country.

Sean Logan, who has worked as the associate director of admissions at Williams College and in the Harvard admissions office, described programs such as the ones discussed in this book as a tremendous resource to colleges that have an explicit mission to expand their pool of historically underrepresented students. Logan sees these programs as a crucial asset in the effort to transform the status quo, where only 8 percent of children who grow up in the poorest quartile of American families receive a bachelor's degree. According to Logan:

> These programs do wonders for low-income kids. As an admissions
> officer representing Williams College, I would spend my time trying

to introduce Williams, but more importantly the idea that college is both affordable and possible for capable young people from poor urban communities. Like other admissions officers, I would schedule meetings at schools. Typically in an urban public school I would speak to one or two students during a meeting, but when I go to an out-of-school program I might be able to present to 30–40 people including parents and staff members. I'm obviously representing Williams, but more importantly and most critically I—like all the people that do what I do—am selling the idea that college is obtainable and within reach.

To Logan, the institutional relationships forged between colleges and out-of-school programs represent a pivotal link on the path to helping disadvantaged youth make it to college. He also believes that participation in these programs demonstrates a level of commitment and drive and a tenacity that colleges want in their students. He stated:

> To be honest, many of the students who have achieved high performance in urban schools in regard to grades may not have the test grades in comparison to private school or suburban school youth. One element that we consider is whether they have the commitment and grit to stick with a challenge. Those youth that join and stay with out-of-school organizations have proven this quality and it's something I and others advocate for in committee.

Recently we observed a novel variation on this theme during our visit to the Urban Squash Nationals held in Boston. When "urban squash" began a decade ago, the skill level of even the best players was significantly below prep school or tournament squash players. At the 2013 Nationals we observed an aggregate of players who are reaching new levels of competitiveness and who, we anticipate, will be emerging on the college scene to follow in the footsteps of those currently at such selective institutions as Bates, Connecticut College, Cornell, Hamilton, Franklin & Marshall,

Smith, and Wesleyan. We suspect that not only will colleges continue to nurture relationships with programs to enhance their diversity goals, but also to fill spots on their squash teams.

An example of this changing dynamic is captured by kids like StreetSquasher Divine Wing. We first met him five years ago as a gregarious, uncoordinated, and somewhat plump seventh grader who was just starting to play squash. By all measures, there was little evidence at that time that he would one day morph into a lanky six-footer who might be categorized as a highly sophisticated and well-conditioned tournament squash player. In fact, when we saw him playing at Nationals we had to do a double-take, as we had a hard time grasping his dramatic metamorphosis. In speaking with staff we learned that early on, Divine had become deeply fascinated by the game and committed to the program, attending practices three or four times a week, year round. During the five years since we last saw him, Divine was coached by a variety of former high-level collegiate players, and competed in numerous tournaments. In essence, he pursued the Ericssonian route to expertise, and the results of his regime of deliberate practice were clearly evident as he won his draw at Nationals against other highly competitive players.

Kids like Divine add to the stature and social capital of programs from which they emanate, as programs are also becoming a source of talent for collegiate teams. This is an interesting phenomenon that was historically embedded in the civil rights movement during the 1960s, when institutions that once discriminated against African Americans quickly came to realize that discrimination was actually counterproductive to fulfilling their athletic goals. Without recruiting African American athletes for their basketball and football teams, schools could not compete with those who did. Irrespective of the social justice arguments of the day, athletic competitiveness was a critical factor in lifting racial barriers to admission.

The relationships being forged between colleges and programs such as StreetSquash have multiple and overlapping rationales. They provide a viable source of diverse students for institutions, as Sean Logan conveyed. But they also are a source of talent that will become increasingly important in filling slots on their athletic squads, in their art studios, in student leadership organizations, and on their orchestras. Thus, colleges and programs have strong incentives to become more closely associated, and by so doing, participants will increasingly find a more direct pathway to higher education.

Consequently, we see that just as affiliations with powerful and prestigious prep schools have historically opened doors to the most selective colleges and universities, so are affiliations with highly regarded out-of-school programs beginning to have a similar function. While graduating from Exeter, Andover, or Choate may tell admissions folks a great deal about a student's academic preparation and prowess, "graduating" from StreetSquash, Artists for Humanity, or Project Coach also conveys much about a prospective student. Having participated in such organizations reflects, at a minimum, a youth's resilience, grit, and conscientiousness, and increasingly, their capacity to contribute to the life of the colleges and universities where they will ultimately matriculate.

WEAVING WEBS OF CONNECTIONS

Out-of-school programs appear to be continuously developing a range of enriching experiences for their kids, from movies and dinners to lectures and trips to workplace environments. From these experiences, youth gain social connections and exposure. They almost never result in a singular transformative event, but "like pennies dropped in a cookie jar, each of these encounters is a tiny investment in social capital."[14] The accretion of social capital happens through a combination of activities, events, conversations, and encounters within program activities. For example, one of our staff members in Project Coach was a graduate of Amherst College. Her roommate was a second-year student at Harvard Law School and was taking a class titled "Race and Justice: The Wire," with the renowned legal scholar Professor Charles Ogletree. This is the course description:

> This course will examine the wide-ranging legal procedures utilized in the highly acclaimed HBO series "The Wire." The readings will

focus on police procedure, criminal codes, crime policy, criminal investigation, drug interdiction, and sentencing alternatives among other topics. Students will get a firsthand view of the manner in which law enforcement officials exercise broad discretion in the course of criminal investigations, and how legislative responses and the problems of crime often lead to dramatic and overreaching public policy. Students will be required to write three short reflection papers during the course and submit a 20 to 25 page paper at the end of the course.

After hearing stories about Project Coach from the staff member, the law student decided to write her final paper on youth development programs and their effort to close achievement gaps and provide positive developmental experiences. In an e-mail, the student described the focus of her paper:

> I've decided to change the focus of my paper to the promise of out of school programs in closing the achievement gap through positive youth development. After explaining all of those concepts, I'm going to discuss a few out of school programs that use a youth development model (including Project Coach, of course), and also examine Cutty's after-school boxing program from seasons three and four from a youth development perspective. To finish, I'm going to propose some policies to promote positive youth development.

We corresponded a number of times as she assembled the research for her paper, and toward the end of her semester she invited Project Coach to join her as guests at a class. It was pretty thrilling. We set off for Boston and sat in a majestic wood-paneled, high-ceilinged lecture hall at Harvard Law School. We heard Professor Ogletree and the chief of police from Baltimore talk about initiatives to engage youth in productive activities. At the end, several of our Project Coach young people stood up and asked questions such as, "What can be done to improve the schools?"

At the end of class we had pizza with our host and she told our teenagers about her own journey through high school, college, and now law school. It was comfortable and captivating. As we left, she exchanged e-mail addresses and phone numbers with several youth. In the van riding home, one of them mentioned that he was inspired by the visit and was really ready to get back to hitting the books after this session that covered schools, goals, aspirations, and perseverance.

Having Project Coach youth descend on Harvard Law School is an example of bridging social capital. Here, our kids made meaningful contacts with a radically diverse range of people from very different ethnicities and social classes. Typically these young people are fenced in from making contact with other kinds of people. They attend schools that are segregated by race and class and live in neighborhoods that function as enclaves of poverty. Finding ways to develop a broader set of connections can be deeply meaningful.

For the young people in the programs that we observed, we saw a widening of interactions as they went from middle school novices to experienced high school seniors. Over the years, they evolved from engaging in their primary network, which included parents, siblings, and extended family members, to making greater contact with community members, peers, and nonrelated adults from different demographic groups. These programs facilitated the expansion of their universe, and with it, the size and diversity of their social networks.

EXPLICIT SKILLS OF BRIDGING CAPITAL

Programs uniformly asserted that they were a launching pad for young people to develop the skills, abilities, capacities, and dispositions that would allow them to bridge to other social circles. For instance, MetroLacrosse identifies two of its five main goals as related to building social capital: "Introduce youth to caring adult role-models who are well-trained to significantly impact participants' futures; Motivate participants to capitalize on the many academic, networking, and career opportunities that the sport of lacrosse offers."[15]

This was a goal of many programs that we visited, and they explicitly taught what Bourdieu would call "habitus"—the socially learned dispositions, skills, and ways of acting that are often taken for granted, and which are normally acquired through the activities and experiences of everyday life.[16]

Programs often enrolled students in workshops or brought in outside people to run activities designed to build "habitus." Kim, the A-VOYCE participant, described a workshop that reflects "habitus":

Anthony and I go to a workshop called the Martin Luther King Summer Scholars at Boston University from 9 a.m. to 11 a.m. every Friday. This week we learned how to put our best selves forward. Here is a list of things that I learned from the workshop.

- Name badges go on your RIGHT hand side, as close to eye-level as possible—never shoulder-top.
- Never ask a senior executive for their business card—they will not have one and it will create an awkward moment.
- Hold glasses in your LEFT hand, leaving your right hand free to SHAKE HANDS.
- Small talk is "huge talk."
- A social introduction is based on age/gender; a business introduction is based on rank/status.
- Always say the name of the most important person first.
- "Hi" is not an appropriate greeting, "Hello" is.
- The social kiss is appropriate in business.
- You show your respect when you rise when someone new enters the room.
- It is better to write the thank you note than to e-mail them.
- Business etiquette rules are the same for men and women.

Programs like the one Kim attends seek to make overt and highly explicit the tacit codes and skills associated with dominant, mainstream culture. Lareau describes how, for middle-class children, these skills are absorbed through an osmotic process:

> In their organizational style, many of the activities in which middle-class children routinely participate replicate key aspects of the workplace . . . Most working-class and poor children, in contrast, have no opportunities for similar employment training. Most of the adults they encounter outside of school are immediate family members or extended family members. Some working-class and poor children interact periodically with adult neighbors, but encounters with adult acquaintances in organized settings are very rare.[17]

Whereas Kim and her classmates attend explicit etiquette school where they are tutored in the "art of networking," young people from the middle class learn these skills and dispositional behaviors in the course of the activities they participate in growing up. We've seen that three forms of social capital intervention can help bridge gaps in "habitus": intervening in institutions within which youth routinely move, such as their schools; helping youth to find their voices and become advocates for themselves; and facilitating bridging connections to organizations and institutions outside of those youth typically associate with.

Intervening in Institutions: Standing Up for and with Youth

Adolescence is full of conflict, challenge, and failure. Even for youth who appear to be impressively successful, the nature of adolescence and school systems present ongoing adversity, continuous pressure, and complexity. Schools, in particular, can be places of obstacles, unfairness, and capriciousness. Young people often have complaints about how they are treated and their relationships with authorities such as administrators, teachers, or coaches, and frequently end up in situations in which they feel powerless. They then need someone in whom they can confide and who can serve as an advocate. This form of social capital is identified by Lareau as one of the categorical differences among child-rearing practices of different social classes:

Middle-class mothers were often very interventionist, assertively intervening in situations. Sometimes parents were successful, and sometimes they were not. But in the process, they directly taught their children how to "not take no for an answer" and to put pressure on persons in positions of power in institutions to accommodate their needs. By contrast, working-class and poor parents tended to expect educators and other professionals to take a leadership role.[18]

We observed that programs take on the role of advocate in two primary ways. First, they often have staff members who are specifically tasked to serve as "professional interveners." These staff members view their role as a supplement or complement to a participant's parents and regularly advocate for youth at school. StreetSquash has evolved a highly focused form of this model. The program's academic director spends a considerable amount of time in the schools every day. She connects with teachers, checks up on grades, finds out about work that is due, and generally troubleshoots any issues participant are having. One of the graduating seniors told us with a laugh, "Tai knows about my school stuff before I do. She is always there. She is always around; you can't escape her. At first it was kind of weird, but then I realized how helpful it was."

Hyde Square has program coordinators whose role it is to make connections at the schools. Yi-Chin Chen, a staff member, explained that the program coordinator sends a letter and visits schools, letting teachers and others in the school building know that they are working as a supporter and champion of an individual student, and if there is an issue, they should reach out to that person. She conveyed:

If there is a school issue our staff person can become almost a liaison between the school and the youth and their families. We would go to school meetings with the parents and the students. If there was a big issue and the parent didn't feel empowered the program would be there, or if there was a direct student academic related issue the program coordinator would be the one to contact the school immediately. I would say the majority of the time the role of the program coordinator was to advocate; to make sure that our young people received the help that they need to be successful.

Finding Your Voice: Teaching Adolescents to Advocate for Themselves

A second form of cultural and social capital intervention involves explicitly teaching participants to advocate for themselves within their institutions. Lareau describes middle-class children as expert negotiators with adults and attributes this to the lessons absorbed by watching their parents manage organizational matters, finesse power structures within such organizations, and assert their own power when necessary. In short, middle-class parents teach their children how to engage with various institutions to satisfy their needs. In contrast, Lareau says, working-class and poor youth are less knowledgeable and thus less able to assert themselves and persevere in getting various institutions to provide services that could fulfill their needs.[19]

It appeared to us that the afterschool programs help close this gap between middle-class and working-class/poor youth. A key lesson taught involves becoming more savvy about how schools work, how to ask for help, and how to advocate for what one wants. For example, a staff member of a squash program explained that they try to turn intense competitive moments on the squash court into opportunities to practice managing one's emotions so that a participant can reason and persuade another of her perspective. "We would say, how would you handle yourself in school if you got so emotional? How can you calm yourself down and still work on asserting yourself? How would a calmer approach help you to communicate to a teacher what you need?" Such lessons are a form of social capital transfer in that adults are teaching Bourdieu's "habitus"—that is, teaching youth how to behave in different contexts in order to leverage what they want and need.

Facilitating Connections to Organizations and Institutions

A third form of intervention involves facilitating connections to other organizations and institutions. Almost all the programs explicitly provide students with support to connect to other organizations that might expand their social network or advance their development. The examples are bountiful: MetroLacrosse helps students who have high promise, but attend historically underperforming schools, receive guidance and support on how to apply and be accepted at prep schools. Zack Lehman was candid about infusing this type of capital:

> I had had such an amazing experience as a boarding school student. And all of my close friends were friends from boarding schools, and all of my mentors in my life had been teachers and coaches at boarding school . . . I felt like it was a very positive outcome if I could help get young people into independent schools through our program . . . We made a real point of giving kids those opportunities and at MetroLacrosse we sent a lot of kids to places like Deerfield. I brought three kids up to Gould Academy when I was there from MetroLacrosse and they've all been great.

Many of the programs that work with middle school students help them and their families select and get access to a high school that is more aligned with their aspirations than where they are currently enrolled. One student we had in class at Smith told us about her journey as a first-generation college student who was attending a Boston public high school where the graduation rate was 51 percent, and where her peers were commonly joining gangs, doing drugs, and becoming teenage moms. MetroLacrosse inspired and helped her to change direction by negotiating a scholarship path to Deerfield Academy. There she thrived, and upon graduation went on to Hampshire College, where she also flourished. She told us that as a Boston high school student, her worldview was narrow, and she had no idea that places like Deerfield even existed. In telling her story, she still seemed quite amazed that an adolescent like herself could have graduated from such an elite prep school. Initially, it was her attraction to lacrosse that connected her with people like Zack, who in turn helped her to see new possibilities that would take her on a very different path. As we have learned from Lareau, negotiating the institutional landscape is something that middle- and upper-class parents do for their children, and many of the programs that we visited take on this role of supporting the complexities associated with social, cultural, and economic bridging. They recognize that getting a young person into an appropriate school is critical to their thriving.

SOCIAL CAPITAL AND PEER GROUPS

We interviewed a young man who exuded "the indefinable, abstract thing called cool." He was dressed in an amalgam of styles, from glasses that would look at home on a physicist to a flat-brimmed hat with jazzy colors, a tank top emblazoned with a garishly colored hieroglyphic, and retro-style Nike Jordans. He smiled and sauntered and conveyed complete ease with himself. His high status in the caste of teens was evident in the subtle deference shown to him when he talked. He had bravado and style, and you could imagine that he could roll effortlessly among multiple social contexts and flourish. We asked him, "What is different between the group that you hang with in Project Coach and the group that you hang with from the neighborhood?" Without pausing he said:

> My boys in the neighborhood, they're like cool and fun, but it's always about the NOW. They care about the now and the moment and that is how they make decisions about their time and their priorities. Here we think and talk about the future and how we're going to get there. We like to kick it in the now, but we care about the future and that is better for me.

When you speak to young people about the role that out-of-school programs play in their lives, they almost always describe their value in terms of how the programs keep them focused on positive growth, making comments like "I would be hanging out with friends" or "The program keeps me off the streets" or "It keeps me focused on my future." What strikes us in all of these accounts is that youth view their association with programs as having a protective function. Participation provides a sanctuary from, or inoculation against, forces and values that emanate from other peer groups. In short, the programs provide a form of productive and positive social capital that—at least from the perspective of participants—is in contrast to other peer groups that would, in the words of one young person, "pull them down."

We started to think about these benefits as a fund of positive peer capital. The programs that we observed intuitively understand this and respond in at least three ways. First, they retain an edgy, frolicsome, casual, and mutable spirit. They don't exude the intense regimented and structured feel of school. They provide ample time for socializing and unsupervised hanging out. They have rules, standards, expectations, and focus, but they recognize that youth come and choose to stay because of the social relationships they develop. Teenagers clearly believe that peer relationships are crucial.

Second, programs provide multiage settings. Schools sort young people primarily by age and grade, and even traditional sport organizations tend to organize youth into narrow age-cohort groups. All the programs we examined include a broad array of ages working side-by-side from middle school through high school and up to and including college students. The intermixing of ages and ability levels suggests that programs focus on developmental growth rather than categorizing children merely by age or grade.

Third, programs provide a vast array of enrichment activities when schools are not in session, such as holiday breaks and summer vacation. Recognizing the importance of such periods, when more well-off youth often gain a differential advantage, these programs uniformly aspire to close and eliminate this gap by infusing social and cultural capital into the lives of participants.

TRAVEL AND BUILDING SOCIAL CAPITAL

We observed that many programs provide opportunities for young people to travel, and in so doing, expand and bridge their social capital. For example, several of the squash programs developed a participant exchange program between cities. Katie Siegel, the director of Beyond Walls Squash in Minneapolis–St. Paul, brought three youth whom she worked with during her tenure at StreetSquash to work alongside her as coaches of novice players in her Minnesota program. For these young players, the opportunity to demonstrate their expertise, serve in an emerging program, and experience a different community yielded a constellation of positive outcomes, including the expansion of their social network. In a thank-you note sent to Katie from a StreetSquasher, one can see how appreciative the youth was to get such a travel opportunity:

> Hey Katie! I am writing you this letter to say how much I loved spending time with you this summer. I know it wasn't for that long but it was definitely an interesting one. You made my summer a whole lot better. From just the wonderful kids and staff you have in the program, the food (especially the Klondike bars), your house, your dog Blu and just the people we met. Despite me getting you a bit frustrated, it was great! When there is anything I need or need to talk about you are always someone I can go to. Being with you this summer opened my eyes. I learned more about myself than I expected to. But there is still a lot more growing to be done. Also being at the fundraiser with the people on the Beyond Walls board was amazing. They are all cool and full of life! You're doing a terrific good! Don't be so hard on yourself, like I am, you'll be fine. I'll be back in Minneapolis sooner than you think. Can't wait to see how big the program gets.

Inspired by the success of the first exchange, Katie did what so many of these entrepreneurial directors do—they run with an idea and find a way to expand it. She organized a return exchange and sent several of her novices from Minneapolis–St. Paul to StreetSquash in Harlem. The youth were exposed to an array of players having different levels of expertise, were coached by the New York staff, met a range of adults who volunteer at StreetSquash, lived with local families, and toured the city. Perhaps most important, they spent time each day working with the director and engaging in hours of sustained conversation about life, goals, and future plans.

Such activities provide multidimensional benefits—a travel experience, an opportunity to meet new people and develop independence, and a whole host of other positive youth outcomes. A mother of a participant texted Katie and acknowledged her appreciation for the travel and educational opportunity afforded to her son:

> My son loves squash more than football and I know he loves football cause he gave karate up for football. I will always be supportive of any program that helps my child become a better person and get the education he deserves.

This mother's enthusiasm for her son's expanded educational experiences and enrichment opportunities is matched by the responses we heard from many other parents, who appreciated that the programs appeared plugged into networks that the parents themselves were unable to provide.

Another example of expanded summer opportunities involves the international trips that some programs offer. For example, in July 2012 several StreetSquash participants undertook a journey to Nicaragua. Again, the idea here is that travel enriches one's knowledge of the world as well as one's self, and creates opportunities to meet new people and build social networks. Here is an inspired post:

> When we arrived in Matagalpa I was immediately excited to explore the community because it appeared more walkable and relaxed than the hustle and bustle of Managua . . .
>
> As we leave Matagalpa, it is not just with our woven crafts and organic coffee, it is with a better understanding of what life is and was like for the people of Nicaragua. I, for one, leave continuing to challenge my own ability to stand up in the face of adversity and hoping to continue to share all the stories I have learned with my family, friends, students, and anyone who will listen!
>
> —Loren

In general, programs work to expand horizons and swathe youth in a range of absorbing and poignant learning experiences that are meaningful and captivating. The preceding examples are jaw-droppingly exotic and expensive, but programs do many things closer to home, too. For example, when Newark mayor Cory Booker came to Springfield, we took our whole contingent of Project Coach adolescents to listen to him talk about his efforts at urban renewal. On another occasion we heard Geoffrey Canada talk about the Harlem Children's Zone. Other programs routinely take youth to museums, the theater, and sporting events. The clear motivation for offering this web of opportunities is the same as the driving purpose behind concerted cultivation. Such activities are deliberate attempts to stimulate development, foster cognitive and social skills, and build complex social networks that not only serve as a resource of knowledge, but also can be leveraged to advance a youth's current and future opportunities.

In our conversations, program leaders expressed deep empathy for the inequities of families' circumstances. Social class differences affecting the quality and quantity of children's activities do not stem from fundamental differences in parents' desires to help their children develop or to cultivate their skills and talents. Instead, these variations stem from parents' unequal access to a wide range of resources, including money, the human capital to know how best to assess and improve children's skills, the cultural capital to know how to cultivate children's talents, and the social capital to learn about and gain access to programs and activities.

We have seen how programs cultivate a vast array of internal and external assets in their participants, but ultimately, how they are utilized and transfer to other contexts in a youth's life is the critical test of a program's impact. In chapter 7, we examine what we have learned about the "transfer question."

CHAPTER SEVEN

The Transfer of Supercognitives
Deploying Skills Across Settings

Everyone believes in transfer.
—JILL H. LARKIN

Some of these kids are stars in our program, but when they get back into the context of school they flounder. I sometimes fantasize about us having our own school, or even better, something like Boys Town, or even better than that—if we could have our own version of Deerfield Academy.
—PROGRAM DIRECTOR

"This is a school?" asked Ricky, one of our Project Coach graduates who now works with us as a supervisor. His nose was pressed up against the car window as we drove past the stately fieldstone buildings, sprawling athletic complex, and manicured lawns of one of the many classic New England private schools that are within a short drive of Springfield. He asked the question with the same depth of incredulousness that I remember feeling driving past the estates of Newport, Rhode Island. "*These* are homes? Like where people live?"

We had been invited by one of Don's former students to present Project Coach to a class she was teaching in sport studies. We drove past a wrought-iron gate and parked in a quadrangle that backed up to a gently descending incline and a small lake ringed with drooping willows. We headed into a building whose modern facade consisted of large glass plates angled into each other. Inside the lobby was a student artwork exhibition with museum-quality mountings. "Wow," muttered Ricky as we walked past sketches, paintings, and sculptures.

We presented the concept and ideas of Project Coach to nine attentive students who sat in a U-shaped formation in a seminar room. Ricky did a superb job presenting how Project Coach tries to serve as a catalyst for community improvement and change in his neighborhood. At the end of the session, the students asked some thoughtful questions. The teacher thanked us and explained that our presentation was one of a series that would include talks by college athletic directors, coaches, former professional athletes, and scholars of sport economics.

As we finished a broad-shouldered young man with closely cropped hair and a varsity letter jacket came up to Ricky and Sam and said, "Thanks; that was really interesting. I like how you are trying to tie everything together: sport, community, coaching, and school. It's sort of what we have here." Ricky laughed easily and scanned the room, taking in the scene. "Yeah, we try and tie everything together," he replied, "but it's hard because we go to so many schools in the city."

Classes must have just finished as we walked back to the car. Groups of students ambled along the quadrangle paths to other buildings. Faculty walked among them, talking with small groups of students. It felt almost as if we were on a movie set. Ricky asked, "So is this a school, like where that kid that talked to us at the end lives here all the time during the year?" We explained that residential boarding schools are places where students live in dorms, eat in dining halls, attend classes, and participate in a wide range of activities such as sports, theater, music, and debate. Ricky grinned and said, "It's like a one-stop school or college."

Ricky's "one-stop school" remark represents a crucial observation with regard to the programs we examined for this book. In our travels and conversations, a recurring theme was how program staff fantasized about securing a windfall donation that would enable them to become a "one-stop" entity providing full-service support for youth. The fascination with prep schools and, to some measure, charter schools derived from the sense that the impact of out-of-school programs is diminished by the fragmentation that youth experience moving between school, family, out-of-school programs, and other contexts. To them, the cohesive prep school system represented a unified, holistic, all-inclusive model that Hicks describes as a "total school environment."[1] The total school environment seems like the answer to the enduring dilemma faced by the out-of-school world: contextual coherence that makes the transfer of knowledge, skills, and values learned in one context more likely to be manifested since the context is all-enveloping.

THE DILEMMA OF TRANSFER

In some manner the entire premise of the educational enterprise hinges on the fragile promise that learning transfers. As psychologist Jill Larkin wrote more than twenty years ago "Everyone believes in transfer. We believe that through experience in learning we get better at learning."[2] That is, if people learn material in one context, we expect they will be able to *transfer* what they have learned, and the processes by which they learned that material, to another context. The sports metaphors "The Battle of Waterloo was won on the playing fields of Eton" and "The way to the boardroom leads through the locker room" convey that what is learned in sports has a critical impact on future, more serious endeavors. Similarly, art metaphors promise that learning to paint or sculpt as a youth means that one will become successful later in life at using imagination and creativity. Although much speculation exists about how sports and arts attributes might transfer, there has been little empirical evidence to show unequivocal transfer.

One recent study in sports does reveal an important finding: Wharton School professor Betty Stevenson recently conducted an exhaustive quasi-experimental study that was able to connect girls' involvement in sports with their future educational and labor force participation.[3] The study separated these participation effects in sports from self-selection effects, which can be attributed to the probability that the type of person who successfully engages in sports would likely also be successful in school and future employment. After controlling for all conceivable variables that might distort the relationship, Stevenson found that a ten-percentage-point increment in female sport participation generated a one-percentage-point increase in college enrollment, and a two-percentage-point increase in labor force participation. Participation in sports was also related to 8 percent higher wages. Stevenson speculated that such things as "the ability to communicate, the ability to work well with others, competitiveness, assertiveness, and discipline," though not assessed, were the critical elements that transferred among these contexts.[4]

The idea of transfer particularly appeals to those of us who work in the out-of-school world. We hold that squash, coaching, art, music, and theater, although perceived as ornamental in the school curriculum, are critical for learning essential transferable attributes. Our aspirations hinge on the assumption that what youth learn in our programs will show up in other contexts in their lives. In the programs we visited, the hypothesis of transfer follows a logic akin to this: if youths master a particular sports skill by methodically and deliberately practicing it, by soliciting and processing feedback, and by persisting despite failure and adversity, then they will apply the same mindset and approach to the learning of quadratic formulas or any other challenges they may face.

When we started Project Coach we ascribed to this same hypothesis. It seemed rather straightforward to us that if our coaches were taught how to communicate, problem-solve, control emotions, focus attention, set and achieve goals, and persevere when faced with adversity—and then taught these things to their players—then they could deploy these same skills in their own lives, especially in school.

During our first few years we taught and assessed how well adolescents were learning this cluster of skills and we also monitored how well they were able to transfer them to their own lives as students. Juan provides a typical example of what we observed. He is a tall and slender high school senior who could easily be mistaken for someone in his early to midtwenties. Juan is among our most dynamic coaches. His communication skills as a coach are superb. He is almost always able to deal with unanticipated problems, and can calm down and motivate even the most frenetic third grader, while keeping a perfectly calm demeanor himself. His teams are typically the most competitive in our league, and also the most sportsman-like. In short, a visitor to Project Coach could easily mistake Juan for a charismatic teacher at the schools in which our program is housed.

Yet, even as Juan thrived as a coach, he failed as a high school student. For the five years he was with us, he was disengaged, disaffected, noncommunicative, and occasionally overtly hostile with his teachers. He failed to complete assignments on time and was on the verge of becoming a high school dropout in his senior year. In short, what he had learned as a coach was seemingly having no impact on him as a student, despite the fact that he possessed an array of qualities that, if deployed, would surely make him a successful student. But clearly, the knowledge and skills that Juan had acquired in Project Coach were not being manifested in the way we had hoped, and in a manner that would enhance his viability as a student. This enigma puzzled us, and we made several trips to Juan's school to observe what was going on. What we found was troubling, although in retrospect, it was not too surprising. Many other students exhibited the same demeanor and behavior as Juan. In fact, if a student acted more interested in what was going on in class, or strove for and attained good grades, this made him very unpopular with his peers. As we saw, it just wasn't "cool" to be a good student.

We learned that environmental incentives or disincentives are powerful in determining whether or not qualities that adolescents possess get expressed. This led us to realize that just as programs need to be deliberate and explicit about what they are teaching kids, so do they need to be deliberate and explicit about teaching youths how to transfer various assets to other contexts.

In contrast to the prep school that we visited, where contexts seamlessly overlap, out-of-school programs must explicitly help participants make connections between the program, school, and the communities in which they live. This is difficult and complex work since programs have control over only one of these environments. While some researchers contend that these varied social and institutional contexts may enable youth to acquire greater social versatility and the capacity to bridge beyond the narrow spheres of their own experience, the prevailing view of those who work in such programs is that the whiplashing between institutions and contexts creates confusion and undermines development.[5] Danish, Nellen, and Owens provide very thoughtful advice on how to best go about bridging between these contexts:

1. Adolescents must be made aware that they possess capabilities that can be used in different contexts. In our example, Juan may not have realized that the communications, problem-solving, emotional control, goal-setting, and perseverance skills that he used regularly as a coach could also be used in school.
2. Adolescents should be given opportunities to practice using these skills in different contexts. Since our recognition of this problem, we now regularly do simulations with role-playing during our coaching classes to help youth learn how they might deploy those skills in school. For example, a coach strives to communicate with each of his players while speaking to them as a group by moving his eyes around, being enthusiastic, and speaking clearly and with adequate volume; the same applies when making a presentation to classmates in an English class.
3. It is important to recognize that taking skills learned in one setting and deploying them in another can create angst since adolescents often feel uncertain of how they will be perceived. Certainly, if Juan were to become the "curve breaker" in his classes by speaking up, submitting assigned work, and getting good grades, he would need assurance and support to make the rewards for doing so outweigh the benefits of following the normative behaviors of his cohorts. While conceptually this may seem simple, in reality it is not. Juan would need to be convinced that morphing into a new identity, and possibly associating with another crowd, would be worth the social disruption of his immediate life, as it might lead to higher education and vastly greater life options than he might have pursuing his current path.[6]

In contrast to the disjointed lives of underserved kids, the resources for a young person attending a comprehensive prep school (where she lives, eats, takes classes, plays, and learns within a bounded community) are shared and coordinated. There the youth develop connections with the adults who teach them, coach them, eat with them, advise them, and care for them. This matrix of intentional programming provides opportunities for the school to formatively influence a young person's development in robust ways. When we spoke to a teacher at the prep school we visited and told him about Ricky's "one-stop school" observation, the teacher said, "Yes. We can develop powerful values and expectations that run through the variety of contexts where our kids move. We can expect similar behaviors and attitudes in the classroom, the dorm, the stage, and the field. We can expect to hold youth to similar standards in the classroom, in our community, and in athletics."

The approach of these schools is designed to achieve consistency and alignment. As the mission statement of Choate Rosemary Hall attests, "Two interwoven priorities define the Choate experience: a rigorous academic curriculum and an emphasis on the formation of character in a residential setting that allows for teachers and students to live with, and learn from, each other in important ways." This holistic view of education infuses itself in the practices and priorities of a prep school—a task made easier because historically the teachers at a prep school serve as residential directors in the dorms, producers of the drama performances, and coaches on the field.

The operative metaphor of a prep school could be gears seamlessly meshing. A typical urban out-of-school program consists of students from multiple schools, diverse neighborhoods, and different backgrounds. Getting these gears to mesh together represents the formidable and enduring challenge facing the field.

Those who work in out-of-school programs understand that the ultimate measure of their effectiveness and impact hinges on whether the young people who move through their program acquire and apply the array of skills necessary for them to achieve success in their lives. The hypothesis that guides this aspiration has already been described: getting young people involved in communities of practice that implicitly and explicitly teach achievement mindsets and skills through engaging activities will have a powerful and enduring impact. This pathway hinges on the elusive promise of transfer.

THEORIES OF TRANSFER

The research literature on transfer is contentious and complicated. Education at the turn of the twentieth century was organized around the principle of what was called "formal learning."[7] This notion posited that training in one discipline transferred to other disciplines. For example, learning chess and Latin were regarded as exercises that would prime one's intellect for other disciplines. Educators called it the "theory of formal disciplines." Thorndike challenged this view that transfer was automatic and ubiquitous by conducting a series of studies that concluded that the degree of transfer between contexts depended on the match between elements across events.[8] In relationship to education, this meant that transfer from one school task and a highly similar task (near transfer), and from school subjects to nonschool settings (far transfer), could be facilitated only by teaching knowledge and skills in school subjects that have elements identical to the activities encountered in the transfer context.[9] Researchers also investigated whether this same principle held for the teaching of character. Hartshorne and May's classic study is often cited as evidence of situational specificity, the idea that there are no character traits (e.g., honesty) that are consistent across contexts.[10] The eight thousand students they studied sometimes lied or cheated, and sometimes did not, depending on the situation.

In other words, learning in one domain does not necessarily strengthen the mind in a way that enables more effective or expedient learning in another domain. Modern incarnations based on the notion of limited transfer, unless elements are identical in two situations, can be found in schools that have narrowed their curricular offerings and reduced or eliminated extracurricular activities. In essence, such institutions are saying that disparate activities have little or no connection to one another, and that literacy and numeracy must take precedence over everything else, since everything else does not significantly impact literacy and numeracy.

A second related view is facetiously described by David Perkins and Gavriel Salomon in their article "Teaching for Transfer" as the "Bo Peep theory of transfer," which rests on the belief that if we teach something in any context then transfer will implicitly and automatically happen—as in the nursery rhyme, "Let them alone and they'll come home, wagging their tails behind them."[11] They contend that suggesting that transfer has such an "osmotic" quality is overly optimistic. They maintain that transfer does not happen automatically. Perkins and Salomon assert that if we merely teach facts about the Revolutionary War and facilitate critical thinking about the sources of war, we should not expect that learning to spill over into other domains of school and life. They cite many studies that describe how one may be an expert in the pure logic of chess, but have no advantage in seemingly related tasks such as solving puzzles or proving mathematical theorems.

This view of learning and transfer would seemingly doom many out-of-school programs, given that their pursuit of expertise is focused on endeavors unrelated to core academic subjects. Art, squash, coaching, music, and other such activities are—at best—viewed as nonessential subjects by schools, and the Thorndike and Bo Peep models of transfer would suggest that youth would derive little that would benefit them in their core subjects. The exception would seem to be organizations that strive to provide an immersion in a field through apprenticeships. Halpern describes apprenticeships as the joining of a particular tradition where youth work and learn in the setting in which a craft, trade, or discipline is practiced.[12] This would describe, for example, the youth who learn to do art in Artists for Humanity and then move on to become practicing professional artists or those who pursue music in a program like Zumix and subsequently work as professional musicians or music technicians. To some extent, it would also be true that the skills developed in sports and music programs could give students an advantage in the college admissions process since colleges use such criteria, along with academic viability, to fill slots on their sports teams and in their various musical groups.

Yet despite the many hundreds of studies that portray transfer as a narrow and prescriptive process, recent research convincingly challenges this constrained conceptualization of transfer. In a much-cited article, "Rethinking Transfer," cognitive scientists John Bransford and Daniel Schwartz acknowledge these perspectives of limited transfer, but propose that transfer can also be understood as the transfer of processes as well as of specific knowledge or skill.[13] They use, as an example, the process by which one learns how to learn, which they call "preparation for future learning." Here, the focus shifts to assessments of people's abilities to learn in various situations. They state:

> When organizations hire new employees they don't expect them to have learned everything they need for successful adaptation. They want people who can learn, and they expect them to know how to use various types of resources (e.g., texts, manuals, computer pro-grams, colleagues) to facilitate this learning. The better prepared they are for future learning, the greater the transfer (in terms of speed and/or quality of new learning).[14]

In today's world, in which industries and jobs come and go with in-creasing rapidity, the ability to learn quickly becomes a survival skill. This understanding permeates many of the programs that we observed. Teach-ing the principles of deliberate practice fits this emphasis on the ability to learn and to adapt to novel situations and problems. As conveyed by Bransford and Schwartz, the traditional transfer paradigms used in re-search tend to focus testing for retention on specific knowledge (replica-tive knowledge) and specific skills (applicative knowledge) that generalize across situations, rather than on invoking less obvious, but more import-ant, thinking, perceiving, and decision capabilities (knowing with). These attributes, they assert, are more tacit and may not be readily accessible for recall and assessment in a traditional transfer paradigm. Also included in their analysis of "knowing with" qualities are affective and social concepts such as tolerance for ambiguity, courage, perseverance, willingness to learn from others, and empathy. In essence, we believe that they are writing about supercognitives, and their importance in the "knowing with" processes is the basis for promoting what we have alluded to earlier (see chapter 4) as the mastery mindset.

The core finding emanating from these new studies is that when educators work to intentionally teach and coach for transfer, much is possible. Here are some approaches that we witnessed within the programs that corresponded to the descriptions of transfer as "preparation for future learning."

Explicitly teach the supercognitives. The researchers on transfer highlight how affective and social capacities such as grit and perseverance, willingness to learn from others, maintenance of emotional equilibrium, the control of attention, and other dispositions toward learning and achievement should be moved from the periphery to the center of learning theory and instructional design.[15] More so than discrete content knowledge or context-specific skills, these dispositions are transportable and can be deployed in multiple contexts. Through what Bransford calls the "lived experience" of learning to play an instrument, learning to perform on task, or learning to participate in organized sports, youth can learn about what it takes to get good at something and about themselves as learners. The critical point is that

> some music, drama and athletic teachers (coaches) appear to help students learn about themselves as they struggle to perform in these arenas. Other teachers seem to focus solely on the performance and provide minimal suggestions for helping students think through important issues such as their commitment to excellence; their need to be in the limelight rather than a team player; their respect for others who are not equally musical, dramatic, or athletic; their (often tacit) fears and strategies.[16]

While some of these capabilities may seamlessly transfer, the emphasis in the literature is on using performance as a "case study" on what it means to improve at something. Asking youth to consider their growth and development in a domain and helping them to understand why and how such growth occurs is what teaching supercognitives is all about. The ultimate goal is the acquisition and retention of a set of qualities that can be deployed in any setting that entails learning new things, overcoming obstacles, and suppressing diversions from staying on task.

By way of illustration, in Project Coach we had a former college basketball player (Ben) who was working with one of our youth coaches. The teenager (Lon) had aspirations of playing college basketball and he asked Ben for some help training. The two met at Smith for a number of sessions. What ensued evokes the larger principle. Ben shared:

> Lon had grown up playing basketball, but he never really pushed himself or trained hard. He never pushed himself to stretch. We worked out a few times and he started to realize what it meant to really work and push. He has improved so much and I think it's because he pushed on beyond his limit and we talk about how the same intensity to push has to do with schoolwork and asking for help and support. I told him, "If you didn't ask me you would never know how good you can be."

At work in this anecdote is the idea that transfer hinges on the explicit exploration of those attributes that can guide performance in multiple contexts. Basketball skills will not transfer to classroom content, but the ways in which Lon was taught to approach the development of basketball skills—with intensity, discipline, and total concentration—are the critical transferable supercognitives. Our observations have led us to conclude that the heart of youth development entails deconstructing, analyzing, and relentlessly teaching youth how to build and deploy the elements contained in these processes. Our claim, which is based on our own practice and our observations of other programs, dovetails with a similar finding in the literature on teaching character education, which finds that initiatives and models that incorporate direct skill training are quite effective. In many cases, direct skill training— for example, teaching listening skills so that cooperative learning can be effective, or teaching peer conflict-resolution skills so that class meetings can be effective—results in transfer.[17] Therefore, supercognitive teaching is, or should be, the core curriculum of out-of-school programs.

Actively coach supercognitives. Identification and deconstruction of supercognitives is not enough. An intentional and deliberate pedagogy must exist to teach them. While traditional hierarchical lecture/discussion pedagogies used in schools can help youth develop explicit skills, such as how to grip a slice forehand in squash or how to use cross-hatching for a background in a sketch, to truly acquire supercognitives youth need ongoing coaching. This entails a coach acting as more of a resource than a director. Such a pedagogy entails guided discovery in which scaffolded problems are presented to a student; then through active engagement and trial and error the learner finds his way to a solution by using and/or developing needed resources. This process, in contrast to the teacher-student/coach-athlete hierarchy that exists within a classroom or a gymnasium, is highly enactive and interactive.

We have seen a great many instances of staff in out-of-school programs coaching youth to work harder, be more focused, maintain emotional control, stick with difficult tasks, and maintain a positive attitude. A few years ago we had a teen coach who had recently emigrated from Puerto Rico. When Juanita joined us she spoke very little English and was deeply insecure about her English skills. She worked wonderfully with our Spanish-speaking children, but was reluctant to speak English in public. One of our special projects involved asking coaches to see the work of coaching as a contribution beyond just the work they did in the gym. Our coaches took on a variety of projects focused on community health. Juanita's mother suffered from type 2 diabetes, which was a scourge in the whole community. Working with, Beth, one of our staff members, Juanita undertook a project to learn about the disease, prepare a presentation for the community, and recruit an audience for the presentation.

Juanita and Beth dove into the work together. They jointly wrote research questions, interviewed doctors from the local medical clinic, and spoke to a range of women in the community who were suffering from the disease. Beth coached Juanita in composing the questions and developing a schedule for the interviews. Once the research was assembled they rehearsed the presentation together and assigned roles to each other. The audience was mothers from the local elementary school, and since they were almost all Spanish speakers, Juanita delivered the talk and PowerPoint in Spanish. Her coach, Beth, stood by beaming.

The point of emphasis here is that just as coaches like Beth help youth such as Juanita focus on explicit skill acquisition related to an activity (here, developing open-ended interview questions and composing the PowerPoint presentation), her more important contribution was participating alongside Juanita and coaching supercognitives. Together they persevered, encouraged each other, and worked as a team that bridged across ethnicity, class, language, and age. Beth coached Juanita in regard to conducting research and producing an impressive presentation, but the real payoff was the emphasis on beliefs about learning, organization, and conducting oneself professionally across multiple social worlds.

Reflect on action and performance. Teaching and coaching need to entail activities that encourage participants to reflect on the processes and problems they encounter while learning as well as on the more explicit products of learning. The literature calls this a metacognitive approach and it emphasizes that a core attribute of learning is to monitor and regulate students' own understandings. For example, youth should learn about their strengths and weaknesses, styles and preferences; demonstrate their ability; and reflect on these various qualities and ongoing processes. Perkins and Salomon describe an approach that has been effective in producing general learning that focuses on preparing youth to monitor their levels of engagement and to manage problems by asking questions such as: Who am I with? What am I doing now? Is it getting me anywhere? What else could I be doing instead?[18] The evidence suggests that having youth work in a feedback-rich environment where they are continually engaged in reflection and self-scrutiny builds the ability to bring that self-critical practice to other domains. For example, in Project Coach, our coaches write letters to parents introducing themselves and explaining what Project Coach is and how it benefits their children. These letters require deeper thinking about what they are doing and why than these kids typically do, enmeshed as they are in multiple activities. In essence, this type of reflection is meta-cognitive, which entails reflecting on what one is doing, why one is doing it, and how goals and actions are related. This aligns very much with Danish et al., who believe that being aware of what one is doing and learning is the foundation for subsequent transfer.[19]

During our travels we once observed a squash instructor demonstrating to a young student the importance of the follow-through in a forehand stroke. At the end of the session he summarized what the student should take away from the lesson, and in reviewing the follow-through, he tacked on the importance of following through in everything that the student did on and off the court. This was artful coaching as it embedded technical skill instruction and supercognitive development into a coherent package. We envisioned the next lesson starting with the coach asking the student what he had learned during the last session, and also asking the student whether he had followed through on everything that he did since they last met.

Expose youth to multiple opportunities to genuinely use supercognitives. As we learned with Juan, transfer of supercognitives does not simply occur through some osmotic process. Youth must have an understanding of the array of supercognitives that they have acquired from competing in a sport, learning to paint a landscape, or playing a sonata on the violin. They must then be provided opportunities to deploy these assets in different contexts in their lives. Most programs do this in their tutoring, community service, and travel activities. In Project Coach we now simulate classroom situations and have adolescents role-play as they are coached to display the same qualities cultivated as coaches. We have also observed youth from other programs serving meals at a homeless shelter, planting trees in urban settings, and traveling to campuses on college tours. While this represents only a small subset of the various contexts they encounter, it is clear to us that program staff continue to coach participants on their communication skills, emotional control, attentional focus, and other supercognitives that were nurtured during core program activities. It is also clear to us that much of this happens implicitly, and that the labels given to such cultivation are not framed as supercognitive development, or any other terminology. Nonetheless, by moving away from their home base, it is evident that all programs feel the need to help youth apply these skills to wider life contexts if their missions are to be fulfilled.

OVERALL, OUR OBSERVATIONS AND experiences have led us to conclude that youth learn many things in out-of-school programs that are unique to the programs and have little transferable value. However, we also believe that many things *do* transfer between programs and other aspects of a student's life. In many ways this parallels what is taught in Zen, in that there are a variety of means—whether martial arts, floral arrangement, or archery—to learn the "great doctrine." But, ultimately, it is the self-transformation, not the acquisition of discrete skills, that is sought and of greatest value. We believe that something similar happens to youth participating in the programs that we observed, and this is where researchers of transfer should be focused.

In a larger sense, transfer can also be viewed cross-contextually. Just as the out-of-school world has learned a great deal from what goes on within schools, so do we believe that schools can learn from what programs are doing well. In chapter 8, we contrast the two worlds, and make suggestions about what schools can learn from the pedagogical practices of out-of-school programs.

CHAPTER EIGHT

What Schools Don't Do

In 1998, two economists and business school professors wrote an important book for Harvard Business School Press describing what they viewed as a seismic transformation occurring in our economy.[1] They contended that we were entering into a new realm where future economic growth would not depend solely on the three conventional pillars of business: trading commodities, manufacturing goods, and providing services. They introduced and defined a new source of economic value: experience. They argued that we are on the threshold of a new era, where if companies want to be successful they will have to stage memorable experiences that will engage and captivate individuals in a personal way.

The impact of an experience should leave an indelible impression, they said; that essence would be its value. It would engage the five senses, there would be novelty and surprise, and each customer would experience his or her encounter with the product as customized and personal. Additionally, those responsible for discerning success would be obsessed with metrics that measure the degree to which consumers described feeling highly engaged in the moment.

In their book, Pine and Gilmore point to companies like Disney as the paragon "experience stager" in that it no longer offers goods or services alone, but a "resulting experience" that is memorable and rich with sensation. "Most parents don't take their kids to Walt Disney World just for the event itself but rather to make the shared experience part of everyday family conversations for months, and even years afterward. While the experience itself lacks tangibility, people greatly value the offering because its value lies within them, where it remains long afterward."[2]

The essence of Pine and Gilmore's argument applies to the programs that we came to know. They understand instinctively that for young people to sustain relationships, programs need to provide not just a utilitarian offering or a goal like getting good at art or sports, but their success depends on their ability to mount activities that provide youth with ongoing experiences that engage them in the moment.

The tricky challenge programs continually face is that if all they aspire to do is provide "thrilling" experiences, they can simply cycle through activities like riding roller coasters, viewing horror films, and having open computer time for students to become captivated by the allure of social media. Programs—at least the ones we studied—have audacious goals for their youth. They aspire to propel youth toward "escape velocity" by keeping them involved so that they can acquire the requisite set of supercognitives that will help them be successful in their program, in school, and as community members.[3] For programs to succeed, they have to create an environment and offer activities that provide intense and absorbing experiences, or youth will find other things to do.

While Pine and Gilmore introduced this work to the business community, their framework borrows from the classic work of educational philosopher John Dewey. A core of Dewey's work from the early twentieth century applies directly to the challenge of youth programming. To Dewey, "every experience is a moving force. Its value can be judged only on the grounds of what it moves toward and into."[4] In other words, it's not enough to have a delightful, memorable time at Bubba Gump's Shrimp House (one of Pine and Gilmore's examples); the essence of a productive experience moves a young person "toward and into" activities that Dewey describes as what "arouses curiosity, strengthens initiative, and sets up desires and purposes that are sufficiently intense to carry a person over dead places in the future."[5] To Dewey, engaging in an array of activities is not enough; they must be educative. The youth programs we observed were rich in these educative encounters, which we believe are the sweet spot of growing up.

Importantly, this theme emerged in many conversations and through many observations. Youth were engaged in immediate, educative experiences. They were fully present and tuned in to what was transpiring. They also were acutely self-aware of how, in many ways, the out-of-school experience was emphatically different from that in school. By way of illustration, consider these two views of one of our Project Coach youth.

In one of the schools where we operate a program, there is a long underground tunnel. Brightly lit by fluorescent bulbs, the tunnel is flood-stained and runs underneath Interstate 91 and a freight train track. Two of our coaches walk alongside a loosely cohered line of third graders as they head from the gym to the cafeteria for dinner. One of the coaches is a twelfth grader who recently enlisted in the Marines. The other is a graduate student from a tony Northeast suburb who played intercollegiate sports for one of the most competitive small liberal arts colleges in the country. In some manner, it's an unlikely conversation dyad, but they are engrossed and comfortable with each other as they herd the kids through the tunnel.

Ronaldo is eighteen years old. Lean, angular, and streetwise, he has been living away from home on and off for two years. At the time of this writing, he has three months until graduation, although according to his teachers and counselors the outcome is very much in jeopardy. Inside the gym, Ronaldo is an energized and charismatic presence. He emanates enthusiasm and a restless sense of spirited good fun. Kids flock to him and his fellow coaches respect his ability to mobilize children and coordinate fun and active practices. In our literacy sessions, Ronaldo performs the reading of storybooks. He uses voices for different characters and exudes genuine fascination with the stories. He also is a quick thinker and has learned to ask open-ended questions in ways that attract the attention of his elementary-aged players. For example, while reading a storybook on baseball great Jackie Robinson, Ronaldo stops when he gets to the page where Jackie begins his baseball career and asks, "Imagine you are Jackie and you step out onto the field; what emotions would you be feeling inside you?"

Little hands shoot up and a conversation whips around the circle. Ronaldo is alert, focused, and taut with concentration and energy. It's a masterful demonstration of small-group facilitation that would stand Ronaldo at the top tier of graduate students preparing to be teachers.

This may strike you as a heady description of a young man about to defy the demographic odds and take off toward a promising future, but turn the camera on Ronaldo in his English class. He slouches back in his chair with his arms splayed in front of him to better show his splashy tattoos. With his posture and a bemused sneer, he signals high disregard and disdain for the class. According to his teacher, he will occasionally exude small snatches of interest, but mostly "he doesn't care and doesn't engage."

If youth development hinges on an engaging experience that lights adolescents' fires, then perhaps the most pernicious and devastating deficit facing American schools is the engagement gap. As Ronaldo described school, "School is just boring and it feels more like for the teachers than the kids." Ronaldo's observation is consistent with the research that continues to show that youth find school devastatingly boring. Numerous studies report on the continued decline in levels of motivation and academic engagement in schools.[6] Other scholarship focused on enhancing effort by students concludes that "all children have interests, motivation to explore, to engage, but not all children have academic interests and motivation to learn to the best of their abilities in school."[7] This work corroborates Csikszentmihalyi and Larson's classic study recording the subjective experiences of youth as they move through their day.[8] They find bleak, abysmal patterns of activation, cognitive engagement, and intrinsic motivation: "Compared to other contexts in their lives, time in class is associated with lower-than-average states on nearly every self-report dimension. Most notably, students report feeling sad, irritable and bored; concentration is difficult; they feel self-conscious and strongly wish they were doing something else."[9]

Disengagement manifests in a range of ways, from apathetic effort on the part of students, to disrespect for the classroom space, to the most visible indication of disengagement: dropping out. A recent report by the Bill and Melinda Gates Foundation designed to investigate what it describes as the "high school dropout epidemic in America" concluded from its focus groups with youth that the single most important factor in why youth drop out is uninteresting classes.[10] A representative student comment from the report paints a dreary picture: "It was boring . . . the teacher just stood in front of the room and just talked and didn't really like involve you."[11] A female respondent from Baltimore said, "There wasn't any learning going on," and another complained, "They make you take classes in school that you're never going to use in life."

This pervasive boredom and frustration with school contrasts with the affection that youth express for their programs. "We have fun in the program or else I wouldn't come," said Ronaldo on another occasion. His synopsis of the program matches the research, which indicates that youth who participate in programs experience more intrinsic motivation, put forth more effort, and feel less apathetic, underscoring the potential of after-school programs as a positive developmental context.[12] In short, they have been able to concoct what Chauncey and Walser describe as a "peculiar mix of factors—relationships, recognition, and relevance, among others—that creates a climate in which students feel engaged both socially and academically and that lays the groundwork to motivate achievement."[13] In reflecting on our time spent with youth and visiting schools and programs, we often talk about how the features of program life could be shifted or implemented in school. Here are several observations.

Schools are compulsory; programs are voluntary. In out-of-school programs, youth vote with their feet. Schools, of course, mandate attendance. This reality hovers over any analysis and comparison between school and out-of-school programs. Young people can choose to attend programs or drop out. Thus, attracting and retaining youth is more of a challenge to out-of-school programs, and they need to offer more of those activities that appeal to youth.

Conversely, the trend in schooling is to narrow academic options and prescribe courses of study. As curriculum has become more connected to summative standardized exams, schools have radically decreased elective courses and other subject areas such as art, music, theater, and physical education. Additionally, while school reform initiatives such as charter schools and the small school movement create more of a personalized environment for students, they also tend to offer fewer academic electives, school clubs, or programs in art, music, dance, technology, and athletics.

These are the activities upon which most out-of-school programs are based, and the ones youth seem to be seeking during their free time. Here, youth have opportunities to take control of their lives by choosing what they wish to do, with whom they wish to do it, and how activities are designed and run. Flexibility and customizable opportunities are the watchword in these organizations since they are not saddled with top-down curriculum constraints and the obligation to prepare students for high-stakes tests. As one former teacher who now works in one of the programs said, "In schools we were so test-driven and standards-based that there was virtually no ability to head off on tangents or create your own curriculum. In the out-of-school world we can listen and follow what our kids most need and develop programming with their unique needs at the forefront."

Schools feel like they belong to the adults; programs feel like they belong to youth. The influential psychologist Judith Rich Harris conveys that years ago she was sitting alone in her house reading a study when she experienced an epiphany that has since become a key idea in contemporary psychology and education.[14] The article she read was about how illegal behavior can be considered a "normal part of teen life" because it is an effort on the part of adolescents to mimic adult behavior.

As she read this, a thought "blossomed like a magician's bouquet" and Harris flipped this long-standing theory, proposing instead that adolescent behavior is motivated by the drive to imitate and learn from the peer group.[15] In short, the teen peer group trumps parental or adult influence, which in some manner explains much of what we see with our youth around both risky decisions and pervasive disengagement in school. Her ideas hold that youth "tailor their behavior to the norms of their group and that the groups contrast themselves with other groups and adopt different norms."[16] In other words, if Harris's hypothesis is right, Ronaldo's pattern of disengagement and hostility can be traced back to his feeling that his school and its culture are proprietary to the adults. In fact, when we asked him what was different about school he said, "In school the teachers have all the authority and the power. In our program we share the power. We think we can change things if we need to and we can talk about the policies. In school, we don't have a real say." In programs such as Project Coach, youth are centrally involved in fund-raising activities, conversations with evaluators, and hosting visitors to the program. These crucial roles that involve "back room" planning around financial sustainability and program quality help youth feel as though they have a full ownership stake in the organization. Conversely, youth who describe themselves as engaged in school are those who are involved in a range of extracurricular events. Involvement and ownership translate into a sense of belonging and academic success.

Schools serve youth; youth are the stars in programs. What distinguishes the organizations we observed are the conviction that youth bring special gifts and assets to their programs, and an abiding belief in the practices that support this view. In other words, youth—because of their youthfulness—can be better contributors to the endeavor than adults. In a widely discussed *New Yorker* article called "The Coolhunt," Malcom Gladwell reported on how whole industries depend on how youth set and create trends.[17] The article described the profession of market researchers who trawl through malls, urban neighborhoods, and parks to seek out what fascinates and intrigues youth and discover how they tinker with clothing and styles to define what is now cool. The goal of coolhunters is to learn how youth adapt products and take that knowledge back to designers, who will translate it into sneakers, clothes, and advertisements that will sell across markets, because youth tastes propel innovation and sales.

In Project Coach, we conduct focus groups with our elementary-aged players and their parents. We once asked a fourth-grade boy what he thought about the idea of being coached by teenagers. He broke into a gleaming, toothy smile and replied, "I think it is PERFECT. Adults yell too much and teenagers know how to make it fun." In Artists for Humanity, edgy and innovative designs emerge from youth who instinctively bend genres, experiment, and fuse art forms. In National Youth Radio, the adult producers rely on youth to identify stories that adults would never realize were important or timely.

Being a teenager is a fundamental asset in these programs. In contrast, English or geometry class is organized to transmit what adults know to youth. The focus of learning inside schools is reproducing patterns of knowledge that have already been designated as the standard form—for example, the five-paragraph essay, or a proof in geometry. Youth design, lead, organize, produce, and play in the programs we examined.

Schools are generally tightly age-segregated; programs provide natural cross-age mentoring opportunities. In 1972 Jerome Bruner, one of the most influential psychologists of the last century, wrote an article titled "The Uses of Immaturity."[18] The article begins by chronicling how primates grow up and then transitions to define the problem of engagement facing "human culture and our species." He contends that "a great many of the world's schools are conventional and dull places."[19] His point is that school tasks have become profoundly detached from the world of natural and productive work.

He further explains that schools have become their own world where the overriding message is its "irrelevance to work, to adult life."[20] The consequence of this is minimal "for those who wish to pursue knowledge for its own sake . . . But for those who do not or cannot, school provides no guide—only knowledge, the relevance of which is clear neither to students nor to teachers. These are the conditions for alienation and confusion."

In this void, youth seek out alternative ways to find meaning and engagement. The most promising is a new form or role where adolescents and young adults who find little meaning in school will "take over the role of acting as models" for younger children. His conclusion is that "letting the young have more of a hand in the teaching of the younger, letting them have a better sense of the dilemmas of society as a whole, all of these may be part of the way in which a new community can be helped to emerge."[21] Bruner's call for structuring opportunities for older youth to have responsibility for younger children becomes a central recommendation by James Coleman's influential report "Youth: Transition to Adulthood" of the Panel on Youth of the President's Science Advisory Committee.[22] The report criticizes the trend in society to create "age segregation among the young." The report's insight is still relevant today: "The relative absence of settings involving age integration with role relations that include responsibility of youth constitute a serious and increasing gap in the experience that society owes its youth. Thus, we believe that future environments for growth should include settings in which older youth can have responsibility for the young to provide an opportunity that is largely missing for youth in today's society."[23]

Schools continue to be highly age-segregated. Age division has intensified as curriculum has become more standardized. The programs we observed were thriving multiage settings composed of youth from middle childhood (i.e., ages 9–11) to young adulthood. Both structurally and informally, the programs provided incentives, expectations, and structures for mentoring, tutoring, and supporting the skill development of younger or more novice learners.

Walking into a Project Coach literacy session where high school students are reading sport-themed children's books to third graders provides an authentic testimonial to Bruner's and Coleman's hypothesis: there is a genuine sense of productive engagement, a playful spirit, and a seriousness of purpose to the proceedings that come from the older youth's feeling of responsibility for providing support and opportunity to younger children. As well, the younger children truly connect with their adolescent coaches.

Schools emphasize individual work; programs operate through meaningful collaboration. The dominant structure of learning and performance in schools is individual. Although schools make use of collaborative pedagogies and group activities on occasion, students are ultimately graded and ranked on what they can do by themselves. The tasks of schooling are primarily solitary endeavors: homework, papers, tests, and in-class exercises. The out-of-school ventures are endeavors of shared and social practice.

The programs we visited all had the vibe of a teeming clubhouse or sprawling family get-together. The multiage cohorts, the informal structure, and the depth of relationships revealed themselves through the frequent playful and teasing repartee. The core processes of the programs involved collaborative engagement, including community planning, shared decision making, and constant feedback. Additionally, programs featured both informal discourse and formal check-in regarding goals, aspirations, and other forms of meaningful and planned conversation. The programs' orientation was what some educational reformers have called a "community of learners" that emphasized genuine interaction. The adults were responsible not for frontal pedagogy, but for guiding the overall process and for supporting youth's shared endeavors. Here, in contrast to school, there was a strong ethic of interdependency in that participants rely on each other to complete the various tasks that need to be done.

Schools emphasize "pure thought"; programs emphasize doing. The cognitive scientist Lauren Resnick described one of the essential differences between learning in school and out of school as the contrast between "pure mentation in school versus tool manipulation outside."[24] Schools emphasize pure thought activities that involve composing, discussing, calculating, and responding. Resnick points out that outside of schools, activities that involve thought and creative design depend on a range of tools that shape and enable cognition. Schools will occasionally allow youth to use computers, smartphones, tablets, books, notes, and calculators to support their work, but—and this for Resnick is important—when the stakes are high, such as for tests and other forms of evaluation, the tools of learning and thinking are eliminated and schools require pure thought.

In contrast, activities in the out-of-school world are more authentic in that tools that help get the work done are, for the most part, appreciated. The goal of work is not to engage in pure "individual mentation" for the sake of evaluating a young person's capacity, but to engage young persons fully in real work. Tools are indispensable for thinking and doing. The world of out-of-school programs is replete with tools, particularly around what are often called twenty-first-century "digital literacy skills."[25] Programs use pictures, photos, twitter feeds, blogs, web pages, video narratives, and more to share their work, communicate with internal and external constituencies, and showcase their successes. These are also the types of capabilities valued by employers, who are more concerned with what potential employees can do than the diplomas they possess.[26]

In all the programs that we examined, youth are directly involved in using these powerful tools and media in ways that significantly accomplish what the Partnership for 21st Century Skills describes as creating media products. The critical outcome the group identifies is to "understand and utilize the most appropriate media creation tools, characteristics and conventions."[27] The tools that youth use in programs are hands-on and minds-on. In the out-of-school world, youth do real work as part of a team as they learn.

Most schoolwork occurs in the classroom; learning happens everywhere in out-of-school programs. Every one of the programs had stories about excursions, trips, journeys, and adventures. The programs had home bases, but there was a sense that traveling and embracing enriching opportunities would provide stimulation, education, and a sense of shared excitement and bonding. StreetSquash would regularly travel to Williams College, Boston, New Haven, and other places. On one trip, they stayed in a house in rural Massachusetts with the parents of a staff member. They played table tennis, swam in the pool, and met a wide range of people who joined them for a barbecue. The program also raises money for youth to attend summer programs at colleges or travel in small groups around the nation and world.

The adventuresome spirit that pervades the out-of-school programs and the informal team building and rapport creation that happens on these trips is a powerful asset. Field trips have sadly become anachronistic in schools as stressed budgets and preoccupation with maximizing instructional time have resulted in the near elimination of field trips from the curriculum. "Local school districts don't have the funds anymore," says Stephanie Norby, director of the Smithsonian Center for Education and Museum Studies in Washington, D.C. The money that school and district leaders once spent on field trips now goes to help students prepare for standardized tests, according to Randi Weingarten, president of the American Federation of Teachers. "In school these days, if people have a marginal dollar, they spend it on test prep because they get regulated there, as opposed to field trips."[28]

School-based extracurriculars emphasize skill development; out-of-school programs focus on positive youth development. In efforts to deepen youth attachment to schools and provide them with a broad array of growth opportunities, practitioners, scholars, and policy makers have long advocated for participation in extracurricular activities, such as sports, school clubs, and out-of-school activities.[29] The prevailing view was that participation is a productive use of adolescents' leisure time while also providing distinct opportunities for growth and development. The benefits to high-risk youth for engaging in such activities were considered particularly important. More recent research has tried to scrutinize this assumption and yielded more nuanced analyses. The cluster of studies examining this question concludes that the potential benefits of participation are subject to the context and to the specific activities.

For example, participating in a basketball program or working as a student journalist doesn't necessarily lead to positive developmental outcomes. Playing basketball requires skills such as dribbling and shooting, while being a journalist requires the ability to interview and write. These skills unto themselves do not translate into positive youth outcomes. As Guest and Schneider point out in their study exploring the link between participation and positive outcomes:

> What it means to be a student athlete or a student journalist or a student council president is not entirely defined by the skills required to execute that role. For example, the structural role of being a basketball player does not vary from school to school; the object is always to put the ball in the basket. But the subjective identity of being a basketball player varies greatly. The structural role is given meaning by the activity, while the subjective identity is given meaning by the context.[30]

This suggests the crucial importance of culture and ethos within a program. The context shapes the nature of the experience. Three important trends are worth emphasizing. First, youth development programs often pick up kids who have "lost" the opportunity to participate in organized school extracurriculars because they have become academically ineligible or have been cut from competitive programs. In other words, kids who most need the benefits of attachment and mentorship end up discharged from school-based programs because of poor grades, attendance, disciplinary issues, or inadequate skills. This is unfortunate because evidence clearly indicates that participation in highly structured programs has positive outcomes for high-risk populations in particular.[31] Second, there is tremendous heterogeneity of programs with regard to their missions, processes, and approaches.[32] While the research base is still emerging, the literature differentiates between programs that strive to develop more intentional and deliberate practices focused on positive youth development, and more skills-based school programs such as those associated with school sport teams, band, debate clubs, and art.[33] Programs like the ones we examined articulated philosophies and missions congruent with the ideas that resilience and supercognitive building are central to helping youth navigate adolescence in healthy ways and that "skill acquisition" is subordinate to the youth development outcomes.

Schools have many formal structures; out-of-school programs are informal spaces. In out-of-school programs, youth and adults spend considerable amounts of time involved in informal discussion and activity. This includes unstructured opportunities during transitions, commute time on trips, and discussions during activities such as video production, musical composing, writing a blog, or practicing a sport. The tenor of impactful youth work is relaxed and interactive. One of the qualities that we witnessed at many programs is conversation that happens as youth and adults work toward similar goals. For example, during a squash drill that involves trying to keep the ball along the wall, the coach and the youth talked about their fascination with Batman movies. Or while preparing for a banquet at Project Coach, youth and staff discussed the virtues of rap, and whether it would be appropriate to use this medium for an impending presentation. In our travels, we observed such conversations occurring all the time. Such interactions, while often off task, are critical for developing the sorts of relationships that lead to productive youth engagement with mentors.

While teachers and students can sometimes find opportunities to talk about issues beyond curriculum and classroom responsibilities, these occasions are more limited because of the press of core academic responsibilities, the number of students in a class, the structure of the school day in which classes follow one another in rapid sequence, and the nature of hierarchical relationships that exist among administrators, teachers, and students. For the most part, such a structure is not particularly conducive to the development of meaningful relationships between students and teachers.

School curricula strive for scope and sequence; out-of-school programs emphasize authentic problems. Out-of school-programs have always focused on messy, complex, and real problems. At Artists for Humanity, the question of how to devise an installation for a lobby involved aesthetic choices, qualitative judgments, and negotiations about style, materials, context, and what Nelson Goodman calls "rightness of fit."[34] The problem of designing the installation was complex and open-ended, and entailed reflective discourse between a number of youth and adult mentors. The back-and-forth of ideas, cycles of drafting possible solutions, and the ongoing critique and feedback loops of such projects differed formatively from conventional school.

While best practices advise teachers and curriculum to work through essential questions and devise messy, problem-based learning scenarios for students, most classrooms work with knowledge in predictable, sequential ways. Tony Wagner, in researching his book on the teaching and learning of twenty-first-century skills, spent time in secondary honors and Advanced Placement courses in excellent schools across the country.[35] His conclusion was that despite the reputations of these schools, students performed mainly low-level cognitive work focused on comprehension, acquisition of information, and reporting back of details rather than engaging in the disordered and complex application of ideas and problem solving.

In a recent issue, *Educational Leadership* (a leading journal in the field) focused on creativity and developing approaches to infuse curiosity, design, and problem solving throughout the curriculum. In the lead article Goodwin and Miller wrote that "to help students gain (or regain) their ability to combine convergent and divergent thinking, educators may need to teach and model how to solve complex problems—such as developing a formula to predict a factory's product costs as its output increases."[36]

This is the type of thinking that is more typical of what we observed at various out-of-school programs. They provide multiple and authentic opportunities to solve complex problems, from designing presentations to organizing sports leagues to training for a squash match or lacrosse tournament. The formidable difference, which young people themselves describe with keen insight, is that such messy and complex problems are a natural and organic element of these programs. They are not contrived or manufactured, but real, high-stakes, time-sensitive issues. As one young man said when we asked him how he would describe the difference between school and out-of-school settings, "In school we talk about Sally buying watermelons that cost $5 and then we have to figure out how many watermelons we can buy if we had $40." He shook his head, "C'mon, we're not going to the store to buy watermelon, but if we have to figure out how to budget for an event that we are running, we have to do the math, and if we don't get it right it's real."

In schools high-stakes tests happen at a desk; in out-of school programs they happen in the public spotlight. An alumna of Artists for Humanity told us that one of the most gratifying, exciting, thrilling, and frightening events in her life was when she exhibited her art. Similarly, on the first day of a Project Coach sport league, coaches have to meet their players, explain how the program works, run several activities, and afterwards greet their players' parents. The atmosphere is thick with anxiety and excitement. At Urban Squash Nationals, a squash player described her feeling as "queasy" as she sat outside the court waiting for her own match to begin. All the programs had routine and repeated occasions for high-stakes, public presentation of their skills.

Many of these events involved being part of a collaborative team responsible for the success of the event. If participants failed, their team would fail. People depended on them, and their performance counted as part of the whole. This shared intensity stoked commitment and focus and necessitated long spans of preparation that was interactive, interdependent, and filled with emotion.

In contrast, though schoolwork typically culminates with a test of some sort, the outcome is generally private. If a student is disengaged from a particular class, or from school in general, a poor grade on an exam has few consequences. Parents and teachers may be concerned, but the student's peers are not impacted, nor does such an outcome affect anyone but the student. This is in stark contrast to much of what happens in the out-of-school world, where collaboration and a public performance of some sort are intricately intertwined. Clearly, participants have more pressure to perform, and from our observations, despite having pre-performance angst, youth thrive on working toward and engaging in these high-pressure situations.

Schools emphasize hard work; programs merge play with work to produce substantive outcomes. Anybody concerned with helping other people gain a skill knows that improvement requires practice and hard work. This holds true for anything—playing an instrument, running track, or writing poetry. Kathleen Cushman's book *Fires in the Mind: What Kids Can Tell Us About Motivation and Mastery* reports on interviews with youth about why they chose to engage and persist in what she describes as getting "really good at something."[37] She concludes from 160 interviews that the secret sauce for getting youth to endure the hard work required to move from novicedom to expertise has these ingredients: "Largely, they gravitated to something because it looked like fun, because they wanted to be with others who were doing it, and because someone gave them a chance and encouraged them."[38]

This formula holds sway in the out-of-school world. Because youth can stay or go without consequence, the programs have to honor the old axiom, "work hard, play hard." Programs that we observed offer playful, informal, even somewhat chaotic spaces where young people can hang out. As one young artist said, "It's just a place to sometimes be with other kids with no pressure." The programs also push and inspire kids to practice and work hard. They oscillate between these two essential elements, integrating both into program activities.

A critical aspect of keeping youth coming back involves the role of the community of practice. The programs exude a collective sense of positive purpose—fun and work are explicitly linked to accomplishing goals, which Loehr and Schwartz define as a "unique source of energy and power . . . it fuels focus, direction, passion and perseverance."[39] They go on to differentiate between what they characterize as a negative purpose, which is focused on remediating skills, closing a deficit, or redressing a weakness. They contend that this purpose is toxic, draining, and ultimately untenable. A positive purpose attends to what moves us and feels meaningful. Said differently, imagine if Artists for Humanity gave this message to budding artists: "You need to stay in our program because you have a tremendous deficit in sketching and creativity. Start practicing." Compare that to the message they do send: "If you persist with your art you can make beautiful things and work with others to create art that other people will want to buy."

Perhaps it is fitting to end with one of our most satisfying moments in Project Coach. Early on in our work, Will Bangs took a course with us on urban school reform. A Hampshire College student, Will was an accomplished musician and had become fascinated by digital storytelling as a medium of communication. He was working on a thesis that would come to use the approach to narrative Ira Glass uses in his NPR radio show *This American Life.*

As part of our course, he became involved in working with our program. While he had played basketball and run cross-country in high school, he was more intrigued by the idea of working with youth around digital tools than sports. He asked if he could assemble a group that would work on a project to tell the story of the program.

Will introduced the idea and a group began collecting images, filming events in the program, conducting interviews, and learning how to cinch together the variety of media into a story. They did this work in addition to their regular commitments as coaches. While programs have themes such as squash and art, they also function as free-wheeling incubators of intense educative experience for youth that often veer away from the core skill. This can happen when a mentor or staff member gets engaged with youth around a topic such as media or music and, in so doing, taps into the adolescent hunger to experiment and tinker with new talents and identities. Will tapped into our teenagers' yearning to tell their story with idealism, creativity, and imagination. He served as an expert who guided their participation, modeled good practice, and kept nudging the group toward production.

They produced a short three-minute video that described the program and how it was meaningful to each teen on the production team. The YouTube link arrived in my e-mail inbox at 3 p.m. on a Tuesday. Earlier in the day, I had received an e-mail from a colleague who worked at a foundation. She was just reaching out to see what I was up to in my writing and research. It was routine networking. I described our fledgling program and pasted the link into an e-mail. Ten minutes later I got this response: "I showed the video to my colleagues. We think it's great. We thought of one quick way to support your operation. We can nominate small $5,000 grants to be funded without any paperwork on your part."

Euphoric, we quickly headed to Project Coach to share the news. The sheer giddiness that ensued matched the emotional high of a postgame championship in sports or the exhilaration following the last curtain call for a play or concert. This was real work that resulted in a powerful outcome. It tacks back to our indelible belief about why these programs matter: when youth become part of a community of practice where they are surrounded by mentors, colleagues, and resources, all focused on work that feels important and genuine, much is possible.

Marge Piercy's poem "To Be of Use" captures the spirit of these programs that we have come to know so well. She writes:

> The people I love the best
> jump into work head first
> without dallying in the shallows
> and swim off with sure strokes almost out of sight.[40]

The programs are communities where people jump into work "head first" and contribute. Through one lens, the goal may appear to be helping young people learn sports or art, but the audacious work is that of youth development—of helping young people become motivated to actively build a positive future for themselves. The poem concludes,

> The pitcher cries for water to carry
> and a person for work that is real.[41]

Youth find enduring meaning in being part of a group doing "real work." That is why young people seek out these programs and their promise of an engaging, personal, memorable, and potentially transformative experience.

About Project Coach

P roject Coach's mission is to bridge the economic, educational, and social divisions confronting the young people of Springfield, Massachusetts, by empowering and employing teenagers to become sport coaches
and academic mentors to elementary school students. We work on some
of the most formidable problems these children face by providing these
crucial elements:

1. A safe and structured environment to join with others who are interested in sports and in helping their struggling community. The
Project Coach environment contains professors from Smith College, graduate students, undergraduate students, local teachers,
adolescents, and third through fifth graders. It is designed as an intergenerational community in which all have valued roles to play
and are committed to learning from one another. Foremost, Project Coach is a family that attempts to welcome and support all of
its members.

2. Paid employment and job training for teenagers at a time when
few work opportunities exist for young people. To become a qual-
ified coach, participants attend training camps and weekly sessions
during which they learn the technical and interpersonal knowledge and skills that coaches must possess. They also develop intrapersonal capabilities that include such things as communications

skills, attentional control, emotional regulation, perseverance, conflict avoidance/resolution, how to give and receive feedback, and how to set and complete goals. Project Coach proposes that many of the same qualities that make one a successful coach are attributes that also help youth to succeed in school, are sought by future employers, and ultimately provide a basis for being a contributing community member and a good parent.

3. Sports programming, wellness education, and sports activities to third through fifth graders who are often at risk for succumbing to a variety of health problems stemming from poor dietary habits and a lack of exercise. Trained adolescents provide leadership and guidance to younger youth in their community by serving as their coaches and models.

4. Educational support to teenagers, many of whom attend high schools that struggle with high dropout rates and low academic achievement scores. Project Coach tracks the academic work of its coaches bi-weekly, consults with their teachers to determine if an individual needs additional help, and provides tutoring twice a week for a minimum of an hour each session. Project Coach recognizes that participants have different academic interests and capabilities, but also is unyielding in its belief that all youth can graduate from high school, and should then have options to enroll in postsecondary education.

5. Literacy and academic enrichment programming for elementary school children. Coaches work with their elementary-grade players to develop academic skills by helping them to complete their homework and by reading sports-themed children's books with them. Coaches, serving as teachers, help to instill in them the importance of being a good role model as well as a sense of empathy for their own teachers. Literacy activities also help them to understand and connect with their players in another context, as they do for players with their coaches.

6. Connections with different types of people and with different institutions. Adolescents regularly meet with college students and

travel to colleges such as Smith, Amherst, UMass, and occasionally other colleges to which they may apply. They are also asked to
make reports to such bodies as the city council and the school committee, and have been interviewed by various newspapers and TV
stations. Project Coach also encourages coaches to become famil-
iar with youth development issues by reading selected articles and
attending lectures given by such persons as Geoffrey Canada, Paul
Tough, and Corey Booker. As well, coaches have opportunities to
train youth and adults from other programs who are interested in
using the Project Coach model in different cities.

7. International travel. Project Coach has engaged in an exchange
   program with adolescents from Marseilles, France. Youth from
   both countries visited one another to learn about programs in their
   respective countries and to build peer networks that extend beyond
   the three-week visits. Project Coach has also had a similar exchange
   with a group of adolescent soccer coaches from Denmark.

8. Venues for promoting community engagement by having adolescent coaches and their supervisors plan monthly community forums during which they organize sports events to bring families
   together. Parents of players and coaches also have opportunities
   to communicate with teachers and school administrators during
   these activities.

9. Counseling to youth who have unique family and/or personal issues. Project Coach has a staff social worker and trained mentors
   who provide support to adolescent coaches for such issues as safe
   housing, food insecurity, drug abuse, and gang violence. Project
   Coach also works closely with a neighborhood health clinic that
   provides youth with medical and psychiatric services.

As an aggregate, Project Coach is an "everything and the kitchen sink"
type of program because its highest goal is the development of each adolescent, and coaching is really just an access point to help youth acquire the
sorts of interpersonal and intrapersonal skills that will help them to thrive
across contexts. As one can surmise, youth embedded in a resource-rich

ecosystem that contains adults, graduate and undergraduate students, an academic advisor who is closely connected with the schools they attend, a social worker who deals with personal issues on a case-by-case basis, and various community people who interact with program elements from time to time are provided everything they need to succeed. Coaches' parents are also encouraged to attend different events and communicate with staff at any time. In the end, like the other programs featured in this book, Project Coach aspires to be the "concerted cultivator" for its participants, helping them not only to negotiate their adolescent years, but also to bridge beyond their local communities and get access to people and institutions that can help them realize a future as part of mainstream America. Learn more at http://projectcoach.smith.edu/.

APPENDIX B

Program Descriptions

Program*	Location and Age Group	What the Program Does
AmericaScores New England	Boston, MA 3rd–8th graders	Provides a blend of soccer and creative writing through writing workshops and soccer practices. One day a week is devoted to interscholastic soccer games against another SCORES team.
Artists for Humanities	Boston, MA Teenagers	Partners youth in small groups with professional artists/designers to design, create, market, and sell art products. With fully equipped, staffed studios in painting/murals, sculpture/industrial design, screen printing, graphic design, photography, web design and video, youth and mentors collaborate on creative projects, many specifically commissioned by clients. In the process, young artists develop entrepreneurial skills and introduce audiences to their voice, vision, and virtuosity.

continues

* We have either visited these programs or talked with participants, staff, founders, or alums of each of these programs.

Program	Location and Age Group	What the Program Does
A-VOYCE— Asian Voices of Organized Youth for Community Empowerment	Boston, MA Teenagers	Trains high school students as tour guides of Boston's Chinatown. Students use their voices to effect positive change in their communities through the power of dialogue and storytelling as they lead walking tours to teach about Chinatown's history, culture, and community.
Bikes Not Bombs	Boston, MA Teenagers	Uses the bicycle as a vehicle for social change. Youth learn to maintain and ride bicycles and in the process, they earn their own bikes and mobilize to become community leaders.
Beyond Walls	Minneapolis, MN 6th–12th graders	Delivers long-term, intensive support in the context of playing squash. Combines squash, community service, and academic learning twice during the week and all day Saturday to focus on personal development.
CityKicks	Boston, MA 6th–8th graders	Afterschool soccer league for inner-Boston middle school students that seeks to engage players and constructively promote self-esteem, teamwork, and fitness through playing soccer.
CitySquash	New York, NY 3rd grade–college graduation	Helps motivated and talented youth to achieve their full potential through an intense commitment that centers on squash, but also provides job training, mentoring, tutoring, community service, and college prep from third grade until college graduation.

Program	Location and Age Group	What the Program Does
Courageous Sailing	Boston, MA Ages 8–adults	Excites curiosity, desire for life-long learning, and leadership skills through sailing. Offers a community that allows youth, the public, and people with physical and intellectual challenges to overcome barriers to access and utilize sailing as a mechanism of personal growth.
Fugees	Clarkston, GA Ages 10–18	Works with child survivors of war and refugees in the United States to develop support and structure in children's lives through soccer. Programs center on soccer but also include afterschool tutoring, a private academy, and an academic enrichment summer camp.
Girls on the Run	Brighton, MA 3rd–8th graders	Builds life skills, individual confidence, teamwork, and relationships through twice-weekly running games. Integrates lifelong fitness and personal responsibility lessons with experience-based running curriculum.
G-Row	Brighton, MA Ages 12–18	Provides rowing lessons combined with mentors, academic support, leadership training, and college advising. Encourages Boston Public School girls to develop both physical and mental strengths and capacities.

continues

Program	Location and Age Group	What the Program Does
Harlem RBI	New York, NY K–college	Joins youth together in baseball teams to coach, teach, and inspire players to become healthy, confident, and active role models for other youth. Also provides academic support to help students enroll in and graduate from college.
Hyde Park Task Force	Boston, MA Ages 6–21	Encourages youth to take personal responsibility for their communities by becoming involved in resident-created community development projects. Through this civic engagement they learn to communicate effectively and maintain positive relationships.
Mass Youth Soccer	Lancaster, MA Ages 5–20+ Coaches	Seeks equal opportunities for youth to play soccer at all levels by expanding access to fields, teams, and coaches; builds and improves skills, confidence, teamwork, and initiative.
MetroLacrosse	Boston, MA 4th–12th graders	Gives urban youth access to lacrosse, a sport not traditionally available in urban areas, and provides high-quality out-of-school programming. Programs focus on instilling fundamental moral values, developing healthy lifestyles, and taking advantage of academic, networking, and career opportunities associated with the sport of lacrosse.

Program	Location and Age Group	What the Program Does
Partnership for Afterschool Education (PASE)	New York, NY	Builds the capacity and strengths of afterschool programs for under-served youth. Raises awareness of effectiveness of afterschool programs, instructs afterschool providers, and advises improvements and additions to afterschool curricula.
Program in Education, Afterschool & Resiliency (PEAR)	Boston, MA	Creates afterschool settings where children can thrive. Advises and collaborates with afterschool programs to effectively use theory and research to maximize potential of both programs and participating youth.
Row4All	Springfield, MA K–12th graders	Creates fun, physically active indoor rowing programs for urban youth in Western Massachusetts. Combats childhood obesity by bringing fitness to urban youth and into school physical education classes.
Spells Writing Lab	Philadelphia, PA Ages 7–13	Runs writing workshops to improve literacy. Combines writing and other artistic disciplines as well as assisting with in-school publications, teacher development, and tutoring.
Sportsmen's Tennis	Boston, MA K–12th graders + high school dropouts	Uses tennis to increase physical activity of youth and teach leadership skills, as well as offering out-of-school and community programs to develop academic proficiency and ensure that participants maximize their athletic and academic potentials.

continues

Program	Location and Age Group	What the Program Does
SquashBusters	Boston, MA 6th grade–college graduation	Engages participants in squash to provide long-term, year-round support through sport, academic enrichment, community service, and college preparation and placement. Maintains close, personal relationships with youth through the program and college to encourage college graduation.
StreetSquash	New York, NY Elementary–college graduation	Exposes youth to diverse challenges, from squash competitions to academic experiences, while maintaining the highest standards. Enrichment includes college prep as well as tutoring, mentoring, and leadership development from elementary school to beyond college graduation.
Telling Our Lives Digitally (TOLD)	Springfield, MA Ages elementary–adult	Works with youth to produce digital stories of their own lives and present them at community events. Instructs youth in using technology, telling stories, and developing self-efficacy through presenting their life stories.
Tenacity	Boston, MA Ages 6–16	Splits time between playing tennis and reading books, writing, and discussion to enhance both physical and academic development. Uses both tennis and literacy to develop self-awareness and resiliency on the court and in the classroom.

Program	Location and Age Group	What the Program Does
Up2Us	New York, NY	Trains coaches to combine lessons in sport and life skills through "sports-based youth development." Coaches learn how to instruct youth to become healthy, contributing adults in a safe, supportive, and fun environment.
Young Entrepreneur's Society	Orange, MA Ages 13–21	Provides start-up capital to youth and young adults to allow them to create their own businesses and jobs. Develops projects to fulfill community needs and in the process, teaches financial skills and job readiness.
Youth Enrichment Services	Boston, MA Ages 7–18	Offers outdoor experiential learning for urban youth. Brings youth to ski slopes and other outdoor sport destinations to develop respect for the natural environment, healthy exercise habits, responsibility and accountability, and self-confidence.
Youth Radio	Bay Area, CA Ages 14–24	Trains youth to produce radio media and journalism. The hands-on, creative experience equips youth with the skills and support to secure jobs and education.
Zumix	Boston, MA Ages 7–18	Encourages youth to express themselves through music and art. Provides music lessons, teaches technical skills, and organizes performances for their communities to fulfill participants' passion for music.

Interviews and Conversations

The following is a partial list of the formal and informal interviews we conducted over the course of the project. We thank these people for sharing their insight, knowledge, and conceptions of the field. In addition to these interviews, we conducted nearly a hundred interviews with current and past participants of programs. We do not include these interviews in this list.

Who	Context
Koby Altman	Pro Personnel Manager, Cleveland Cavaliers
Megan Bartlett	Director, Center for Sport-Based Youth Development—Up2Us
Jeff Beedy	Founder, SportsPlus
Richard Berlin	Executive Director, Harlem RBI
Brent Bode	Head Novice Coach, Community Rowing Boston
Steven Bradley	Vice President, Baystate Health Systems
Pat Brandis	Executive Director, Barr Foundation
Art Carrington	Founder, Art Carrington Tennis Academy
Yi-Chin Chen	Deputy Director, Hyde Square Task Force
Carol Christ	President, Smith College

continues

Who	Context
Amy Christie	Network Director, Achievement First Public Charter School
Kayleigh Colombero	Program Director, Project Coach
Kim Dawson	Former Program Director, Zumix
Mike Dean	Health and Wellness Director, Boston YMCA
Rahn Dorsey	Evaluation Director, Barr Foundation
Tim Garvin	Former Executive Director, Central Branch of YMCA, Greater Boston
Curt Hamakawa	Professor, Department of Sport Management, Western New England University
Dana Hanson	Academic Director, Beyond Walls
Emily Helm	Former Executive Director, MetroLacrosse
Abe Henderson	Educator/teacher/artist and coordinator/case manager, Institute for the Study and Practice of Nonviolence
Chris Hickey	Executive Director, National Council for Accreditation of Coaching Education
Anthony Hill	Professor, Springfield College School for Social Work
Liat Hoffman	Former staff member, Bikes not Bombs
Carro Hua	A-VOYCE program graduate
Rick Jackson	Cofounder and Senior Fellow, Center for Courage & Renewal
Marion Kane	Former Executive Director, Barr Foundation
Rob Kunzman	Former high school basketball coach and Associate Dean of Teacher Education, Indiana University
Zachary Lehman	Former Executive Director, MetroLacrosse
Richard Lerner	Director, Institute for Applied Research in Youth Development, Tufts University
Sean Logan	Director of College Counseling, Phillips Andover Academy
Chris Lynch	Former Youth Sports Coordinator, Boston

Who	Context
John Maconga	Executive Director, AmericaScores Boston
Rob Maitra	Program Director, Harlem RBI
Courtney Martin	Author (Do It Anyway: A Generation of Activists) and researcher
Bill McBride	Assistant Athletic Director, Amherst College
John McCrann	Math teacher, Bronx Lab High School
Sean Milbier	Assistant Coach, Western New England University women's soccer team
Ken Miller	Executive Director, Educational Partnerships at Kaplan K12 Learning Services
Ellen Minzner	Director, Outreach Community Rowing Boston
Luma Mufleh	Executive Director, Fugees
Gil Noam	Director, Program in Education, Afterschool & Resiliency (PEAR) at Harvard University.
Ellen O'Connell	Managing Director, Partnership for After School Education
Vanessa Otero	Former Director, North End Campus Coalition
Alison Overseth	Executive Director, Partnership for After School Education
Vanessa Pabon	Founder, TOLD (Telling Our Lives Digitally)
Elisabeth Pauley	Program Director—Education, The Boston Foundation
Sareen Pearl	Program Director, StreetSquash
George Polsky	Executive Director, StreetSquash
Sage Ramadge	Director of Strategic Development, StreetSquash
John Risley	Executive Director, Kate Risley Foundation
Jimmy Rivera	Supervisor, Springfield Parks and Recreation Department
Susan Rodgerson	Executive Director, Artists for Humanity
Greg Rosnick	Assistant Coach, Haverford men's basketball program

continues

Who	Context
Don Sabo	Senior Sport and Health Policy Advisor, Woman's Sports Foundation
Jeff Scavron	Director, Baystate Community Health Clinic
Katie Siegel	Executive Director, Beyond Walls
Mike Singleton	Executive Director, Mass Youth Soccer
Lissa Soep	Senior Producer and Research Director, Youth Radio
Mike Soucy	Varsity Soccer Coach, Northampton High School
Erin Sprong	Rowing Director, Pioneer Valley Riverfront Club
Thomas St. Clair	Trustee, Amelia Peabody Foundation
Ann Strong	Former Executive Director, CityKicks
Jason Talbot	Studio Director/Video Mentor, Artists for Humanity
Marquis Taylor	Founder, Coaching for Change
Kathleen Traphagen	Traphagen Educational Consulting
Mary Walachy	Executive Director, Irene E. & George A. Davis Foundation
Colleen Walsh	Director of Physical Education, Health, and Family and Consumer Sciences, Springfield Schools
Andrew Wood	Former Program Director, Project Coach
Chip Wood	Cofounder, Northeast Foundation for Children, and developer of the Responsive Classroom
Greg Zaff	Executive Director, SquashBusters
Margot Zalkind	Executive Director, Row4All

Notes for New Staff Members

*As summer turns toward fall, we welcome a new cohort of staff
to Project Coach. We wrote this document to distill what we have
learned through our experiences in Project Coach and through the
many conversations, observations, and interactions we have had
with staff, leaders, and youth participants in the out-of-school
world. This memo encapsulates the core principles animating our
program and describes how new staff can contribute to the mission
of our youth development work. Although Project Coach focuses on
coaching, our quest to be a positive youth development program is
shared by all our colleagues in this emerging field, and we felt our
"Notes to New Staff" would be useful to others.*

Dear New Colleagues:

Welcome to our team. On the surface we may appear to be a sports
program, but our ambitious and audacious mission stretches beyond athletics. *We seek to help children and teenagers grow into successful young adults.*

Simply put, this is a daunting task. Many of the young people we work
with come from complex circumstances. They have grown up poor and attend schools with large numbers of underperforming students; in Springfield, about 55 percent of students graduate from high school in four years.
After school, they mostly return home to neighborhoods where the systemic challenges of concentrated poverty—including high crime rates,
gang activity, poor housing, substandard health care, and limited access to

job opportunities—take their toll. Based on demographics, only about 8 percent of the young people who participate in our program would be expected to graduate from college.

Despite the underdog odds, we hold to our defining objective—to help every young person who moves through our program graduate from high school, get into college, and ultimately graduate from college. We know there is chatter about whether college is "right" for every young person. However, our view is that every young person who participates in Project Coach should at least have this option. Foreclosing on it in middle school or the early high school years, before a youth has considered such a possibility, seems unjustified, and may cut off future opportunities that the child was not in a position to foresee.

We strive to defy long odds and we can do that only with your commitment and talents. A long and impressive line of empirical research has investigated those factors that most promote student academic achievement. These studies unequivocally reveal that the quality of the teacher is the single most crucial in-school factor linked to how well students grow academically. In other words, teachers make the difference inside of school. We believe the same is true in the out-of-school context. As the adults in the out-of-school setting, you exert the same critical influence through the relationships you cultivate, the activities you plan, the expectations you set, and the fidelity with which you follow through. In a sense, you are the hinge upon which all else swings.

We're counting on you. There is no "secret sauce," although we believe in three fundamental principles:

- Your personal presence and way with young people count—a lot!
- Youth need adults who care for them and help keep them organized.
- You must learn to teach youth how to become successful adults.

WHO YOU ARE MATTERS!

There is no special rulebook or incantation to working with youth in the out-of-school context. So much of the work flows through your personal qualities. As Parker J. Palmer, a well-known educational philosopher observes,

> The secret is hidden in plain sight: good teaching cannot be reduced to technique; good teaching comes from the identity and integrity of the teacher. In every class I teach, my ability to connect with my students, and connect them with the subject, depends less on the methods I use than on the degree to which I know and trust my selfhood—and am willing to make it available and vulnerable in the service of learning.[1]

Good youth workers possess the same capacity. They weave connections between themselves, the youth, and the larger world. Once the relationship is sound, the learning that can be accomplished can be transformative and distinct from what a young person might be experiencing in other areas of life, such as school.

Your passion for young people, your energy to get them excited about their future, and your own record of diving in and becoming animated by your own activities are why we hired you. Passion is a quality notoriously difficult to pin down, but it shows in the way your teaching inspires students and in the intensity of your commitment.

While passion often connotes an inner fire, you must find ways to spark similar interest among young people. There are people whose enthusiasm for art, writing, or sport drives their performance in quiet and private ways. We honor this type of expression, but for you to thrive in our program and impact young people, you must be able to invoke excitement for the task at hand in those who play for you. John Wooden—perhaps the most revered and successful college basketball coach in history—has written extensively about his intentional efforts to coach life lessons to his players. He writes, "As a leader, you must be filled with energy and eagerness, joy and love for what you do."[2] We view our program as a community of practice and we believe that, like any intensive community, we are vulnerable to contagion. When a staff member brings energy and excitement to the community, we all get "infected" by that heat and drive. Conversely, lethargy and cynicism can infect us in ways that derail our best aspirations for the work.

Clearly, we want staff who are "fully there" when they arrive at our program. In sport they call it "game time"; in drama and music it's "show time." When you show up, we ask that you come prepared to channel all of your energies into the physical, cognitive, and emotional labors of the work.

TEACH ABOUT SUCCESS, BOTH EXPLICITLY AND IMPLICITLY

Passion and enthusiasm without direction would just be random energy. We are a community of practice singularly devoted to fostering the development of the skills and talents of the youth in our program. As a staff member who has experienced success in your own life, we hope that you can teach and reinforce those critical lessons that cultivate success. We hold to the idea that the skills related to achievement are profoundly malleable. As the psychologist Heidi Grant Halvorson writes:

> Research tells us it's using the right *strategies* that leads to accomplishment and achievement. Sounds simple, but strategies like being committed, recognizing temptations, planning ahead, monitoring your progress, persisting when the going gets tough, making an effort, and perhaps most important *believing you can improve,* can make all the difference between success and failure.[3]

Her premise is inspiring: we can help young people learn these strategies of success. She and others believe that youth need to be inspired and aspire to worthwhile goals. They need to have realistic strategies for reaching them, and ways to deploy such tactics in their day-to-day lives. As well, they need you to be their support system to help them stay "on the rails," or to reengage when they go off track. Changing behavior and building internal and external assets is not easy, but for young people who remain committed to our program, success will come.

We have many explicit lessons that teach kids the rudiments of success, but even more important are the implicit ways that they learn these things from being part of our community and culture. We all believe that when each of us commits to doing "whatever it takes" to help kids thrive, the community becomes stronger, and the youth who live in it come to internalize the values we promote and lessons we teach. Being part of this process is ennobling, and shows us all how providing equal opportunity to those who are disproportionately underserved can "level the playing field" and enable them to compete with those who have had many more advantages.

HELP YOUNG PEOPLE LEARN TO MANAGE
AND CONTROL THEIR LIVES

The ability to manage one's self is encompassed by the umbrella concept of self-regulation or self-control. It includes the ability to concentrate, to overcome counterproductive impulses, to work autonomously, and to restrain oneself when tempted by various diversions. The good news is that self-regulatory skills can be acquired. In fact, under the right kinds of instruction—including appropriate guidance, modeling of effective strategies, and creating supportive and challenging contexts—they have been found to be quite malleable. We believe that Project Coach activities are uniquely suited to promote this type of learning for the following reasons.

First, an optimal condition for developing and honing self-regulation occurs when youth can set their own goals and pursue meaningful experiences of their own volition. As a voluntary activity, Project Coach provides young people with many opportunities to make choices about what they do, how they will do it, and with whom. Over the years we have learned that when youth are given such decision-making authority, they are more likely to adhere to the decisions they make and to fulfill the commitments they have made to one another and to the program. In essence, youth learn self-regulation from being given opportunities to self-regulate. We see your job as nurturing this process, and providing guidance to our youth when the complexities in their lives divert them from fulfilling their goals.

Second, our community values giving and receiving forthright feedback. In learning to coach a sport, our youth learn to provide feedback to their players on their performance, effort, and behavior as team members and competitors. Similarly, they come to learn how important feedback is to their own lives, and to fulfilling their short-and long-term goals. Consequently, as their mentor and coach, you will help them learn to use feedback to become better coaches, students, and community members. In essence, this builds their self-regulatory capacities by teaching them that feedback is the fuel that allows them to improve on whatever task they choose.

Third, youth in Project Coach work on an array of complicated activities that require tremendous attention and focus over long periods of time. Not only do they coach sports, but they also read books with their teams, produce videos about the program and themselves, and participate in community forums. These activities are demanding and require sustained attention and devotion. By following through on such endeavors they learn to be responsible, to disregard diversions, to multitask, and to marshal their considerable energy. Again, you are intricately involved in working with our coaches on these projects, keeping them on track, and providing both technical and emotional support.

Fourth, a youth's emotions often rise or fall depending not only on things that happen at Project Coach, but on events that occur at school, with their friends, or at home. We also know that adolescence is a very challenging time when hormones rage, decisions get made impulsively, and bodily changes can make youth feel self-conscious. Nonetheless, in the midst of such internal disequilibrium, they still need to perform the tasks for which they are responsible. Here, you will play the role of counselor. While we teach coaches techniques to help their players control their emotions, we also want you to help them learn to use these techniques in other activities in which they engage. By possessing such skills and understanding how to apply them in different contexts, youth will gain another level of control over themselves that will pay dividends as they encounter unforeseen challenges.

HELP KIDS ASSEMBLE NETWORKS OF SUPPORTERS, MENTORS, AND CHEERLEADERS

The youth you will work with mostly live and interact with others within a closed loop of their neighborhood and school. They rarely circulate with young people outside of their social and ethnic group in ways that can advance their aspirations or create connections that can lead to jobs, enrichment opportunities, or novel learning experiences. One of the greatest assets that you bring to Project Coach is your social capital, which relates to the people and networks to which you are connected. Another way to think about this role is to conceive of yourself as a bridge to another world for youth who have been literally and metaphorically isolated from people and places that can provide them with many unforeseen opportunities. We challenge you to think about all of the people in your life who have helped you to achieve the things you have accomplished, and to think of ways that you can provide Project Coach participants with similar contacts.

A number of years ago we assembled a group of twenty coaches in a room and asked them how many knew someone who was in college. To our surprise, only one hand was raised, and when we asked that individual more about the acquaintance, we learned that the connection was very vague, and the details of where that person went to college were even more so. Think how difficult it would be for such kids to plot a college path, stay on it, and when the time came, complete an application and financial aid forms on their own. You will be their lifeline to pursuing this route. Having recently negotiated all these hurdles yourself, we are hoping that you can serve as a guide, mentor, and resource center for helping them also reach the finish line.

TEACH THEM HOW TO BE POWERFUL COMMUNICATORS

When our young people stand up before new staff and ask, "What do you think we—the teenagers—look for in a perfect staff member?" they do so with the poise and assurance that comes with many hours of practice being communicators. We have found that in survey after survey, employers report that it is difficult to find the competent, creative workers they need to compete in the global economy. Employers explain that they seek workers who can not only read and write, but also solve problems, work on diverse teams, utilize technology, and flexibly adapt to new challenges. A particular area of concern involves the fundamental skills of communication and presentation. At Project Coach, we value all of these attributes, but view communication skills as the hub for all the others. By communication skills, we mean the ability to articulate thoughts and ideas clearly, whether one on one, to small groups, or in public forums. Because school is often so highly regimented and driven by the need to coordinate large groups, young people seldom get opportunities to engage in these types of interaction. At Project Coach, on the other hand, "communication" can involve everything from giving formal presentations to unfamiliar and cross-generational groups to making motivational pitches to uninspired and often disrespectful young children. For coaches, communications skills are the foundation upon which everything else depends, and we think that this is also true for excelling as a student or, subsequently, as an employee or employer. As staff, you have many opportunities to help young people rehearse and deploy their communication skills. Here are two explicit ways that you can help them grow in this essential skill.

Model effective communication in your interactions with youth. Because you spend much of your time working alongside youth, you have numerous opportunities to model what it means to ask questions, actively listen, and rehearse for formal presentations. As they participate with you in these communication events, they will absorb important lessons. The more overt and less tacit you make your thinking, the clearer the learning will be. An important practice to adapt is to "think aloud." Explicit modeling demystifies what can often be understood as a tacit process.

Work with coaches to recognize how different contexts require different forms of expression. We recognize that our teens like to "kick back" and hang out in our program, but we reinforce the crucial capacity to "flip the switch," a term that Greg Rosnick, a former staff member, shared with us. He meant the ability to adapt your behavior and presentation to convey the appropriate impression to the people you are with. How you communicate with friends in informal settings is different from how you should communicate in school, and this may differ from how you might interact with adults at a formal social setting. The ability to read the social cues in a situation and modulate behavior involves high levels of self-awareness and self-management. The takeaway is that programs such as Project Coach provide stimulating opportunities to practice these skills, and we hope that you can play a part in finding the "teachable moments" to facilitate learning.

"KEEP ME ORGANIZED AND CARE ABOUT ME!"

As program directors, we believe all of the preceding goals are crucial, and so do the youth who participate in our programs. As we often do in our work, we try and listen to what youth have to say about their own lives and circumstances. Here is what they tell us they want from you as a staff member:

- "We want you to respect us and to take the time to learn about who we are, what we've done, and what we dream about."
- "Help me to be organized and not screw up."
- "Believe in me."
- "Help me find my way."

From these statements, one can readily see that they want to do the right thing, and they really want you to help them. They want you to listen to them, respect them, ask them questions, trust them, and not give up on them. While this list may seem straightforward, a confounding factor in your understanding their pleas is the probability that you have had a very different childhood and adolescence. You may be of a different socioeconomic class, be of a different racial or ethnic group, and come from a different geographical region. Most certainly, your experience with schools and your educational accomplishments are not the norm for our kids. You have much learning to do in your quest to really fulfill what these kids want from you. In essence, they want a dependable, supportive, and committed ally in the journey of growing up. You can become one if you come to this work with an open mind, are willing to learn from them, show empathy for their plight, possess the necessary degree of humility, can maintain a sense of humor, and above all, be patient with them.

SOME PRACTICAL SUGGESTIONS

You are on board and ready to go. Here are some concluding thoughts to help get you "off the deck" once you begin:

1. *Do your best work in the minutes before sessions begin, during transitions, and during downtime.* Unscheduled time is an opportunity for informal conversations. It's a time to check in, ask questions, listen in on conversations, and generally pick up on things that are important for you to know as a mentor, educator, and ally. Many times staff will congregate among themselves and miss out on the opportunity to pick up information or build connections and trust.

2. *Never turn down van time.* Driving kids around means that you are a captive audience, as are the youth. It's a time to talk, laugh, ask questions, and tell stories. Van time provides opportunities to just hang with a captive audience. It is really amazing what gets discussed during these times and what you can learn.

3. *Help with essays or applications.* When students have to apply for a summer program or to college, the essay matters. Former staff consistently conveyed to us how helping an applicant come up with a poignant, meaningful topic resulted in access to aspects of a young person's personal story that would normally be difficult to glean.

4. *Show up at their games, concerts, performances, or other events.* We encourage staff to go to our kids' football games, concerts, and the like. There is symbolic power in this gesture, but it also presents an opportunity to see youth in a different context.

5. *Stay connected with your colleagues.* Resist the urge to merely "do your own thing." The problems that we face are too thorny and complex. Work with other staff as a team, learn from each other, and support one another when challenges emerge that appear insurmountable. We urge you to think of ways to "go over, under, or through obstacles" together. It is really amazing when you can draw strength from the group, and not feel as if all your problems need to be resolved by you alone.

6. *Share your knowledge.* Youth development is an emerging field. Even those folks who have worked in the field for many years remain humble, and readily convey that we are still only beginning to understand how best to do this work. There are exciting opportunities to contribute to building knowledge in the field and discovering best practices. Attend conferences, write about your work, and get involved in professional networks.

7. *Tend your love of the domain.* If you were hired because you were a college squash player or a visual arts major in college, keep making your art or playing your sport. Aside from deriving personal satisfaction from doing what you love, you'll convey your passion to the young people you mentor. We model commitment and devotion to a craft when we keep up our habits of training or attachment. Passion for an activity is contagious, and is often an access point for kids who know little about the core activity of a program.

8. *Resist the minutiae.* The longer you stay involved with an organization, the more you'll get asked to take on administrative tasks. These can be event organizing, project management, grant writing, or other tasks that are part of running various operations. While these activities are worthy endeavors, and essential to the health of an organization, make certain that they do not diminish the time and attention you give to the kids. Like a good parent, always make their needs and well-being the priority.

Between us we have worked for over sixty-five years in education. During this time we have learned that there are many unknowns when working with youth. However, always thinking about their interests first, and learning to empathize with the reasons for their behavior—irrespective of how rational or irrational you may think it is—will usually get you to the right place. We both believe that out-of-school organizations, more than any other setting, are a place for life-changing work.

Sincerely,
Sam Intrator and Don Siegel
Smith College and Project Coach

NOTES

Preface

1. Luis is a pseudonym, as are all names of young people in this book.

Introduction

1. Massachusetts Department of Education, *School Panel Review Report: Gerena Community School* (Medford, MA: Massachusetts Department of Education, 2003).

2. Tony Wagner, *The Global Achievement Gap: Why Even Our Best Schools Don't Teach the New Survival Skills Our Children Need—and What We Can Do About It* (New York: Basic Books, 2008), 339.

3. Richard Rothstein, *Class and Schools: Using Social, Economic, and Educational Reform to Close the Black-White Achievement Gap* (Washington, DC: Economic Policy Institute; New York: Teachers College Press, 2004).

4. Ibid., 86.

5. Robert Halpern, *The Means to Grow Up: Reinventing Apprenticeship as a Developmental Support in Adolescence* (New York: Routledge, 2009); R. W. Larson, "Positive Development in a Disorderly World, " *Journal of Research on Adolescence* 21, no. 2 (2011): 317–334; Joseph E. Zins et al., *Building Academic Success on Social and Emotional Learning: What Does the Research Say?* (New York: Teachers College Press, 2004).

6. Lauren Sosniak, "The 9% Challenge: Education in School and Society," *Teachers College Record*, May 2001.

Chapter One

1. http://blog.masslive.com/breakingnews/2007/09/springfield_no_6_for_child_pov.html.

2. Greg J. Duncan and Richard J. Murnane, eds., *Whither Opportunity? Rising Inequality, Schools, and Children's Life Chances* (New York: Russell Sage Foundation, 2011).

3. Sean F. Reardon, "The Widening Academic Achievement Gap Between the Rich and the Poor: New Evidence and Possible Explanations," in *Whither Opportunity?*, Duncan and Murnane, 1.

4. Gerald Haigh, "To Be Handled with Care," *The (London) Times Educational Supplement*, sec. 4, February 10, 1995.

5. Duncan and Murnane, *Whither Opportunity?*; Chester E. Finn, *Troublemaker: A Personal History of School Reform Since Sputnik* (Princeton, NJ: Princeton University Press, 2008).

6. Finn, *Troublemaker*; Grover J. Whitehurst and Michelle Croft, *The Harlem Children's Zone, Promise Neighborhoods, and the Broader, Bolder Approach to Education* (Washington, DC: Brown Center on Education Policy at Brookings, 2010).

7. Richard Rothstein, *Class and Schools: Using Social, Economic, and Educational Reform to Close the Black-White Achievement Gap* (Washington, DC: Economic Policy Institute; New York: Teachers College Press, 2004), 210.

8. Reed W. Larson, "Toward a Psychology of Positive Youth Development," *American Psychologist* 55, no. 1 (2000): 170.

9. Jacquelynne Eccles and Jennifer Appleton Gootman, *Community Programs to Promote Youth Development* (Washington, DC: National Academy Press, 2002).

10. Amy Bohnert, Jennifer Fredricks, and Edin Randall, "Capturing Unique Dimensions of Youth Organized Activity Involvement: Theoretical and Methodological Considerations," *Review of Educational Research* 80, no. 4 (2010): 584.

11. M. Csikszentmihalyi, "Intrinsic Motivation and Effective Teaching: A Flow Analysis," in *Teaching Well and Liking It: Motivating Faculty to Teach Effectively*, ed. J. L. Bess (Baltimore, MD: Johns Hopkins University Press, 1997), 72; Carol S. Dweck, *Mindset: The New Psychology of Success* (New York: Ballantine Books, 2008), 277; Walter Doyle, "Curriculum and Pedagogy," in *Handbook of Research on Curriculum*, ed. Philip W. Jackson (New York: Macmillan Publishing, 1992).

12. C. A. Farrington et al., *Teaching Adolescents to Become Learners: The Role of Noncognitive Factors in Shaping School Performance: A Critical Literature Review* (Chicago: University of Chicago Consortium on Chicago School Research, 2012); Paul Tough, *How Children Succeed: Grit, Curiosity, and the Hidden Power of Character* (Boston: Houghton Mifflin Harcourt, 2012).

13. Lois Weis and Greg Dimitriadis, "Dueling Banjos: Shifting Economic and Cultural Contexts in the Lives of Youth," *Teachers College Record* 110, no. 10 (2008), 1.

14. Clea A. McNeely, James M. Nonnemaker, and Robert W. Blum, "Promoting School Connectedness: Evidence from the National Longitudinal Study of Adolescent Health," *Journal of School Health* 72, no. 4 (2002): 138; Laurence D. Steinberg, B. Bradford Brown, and Sanford M. Dornbusch, *Beyond the Classroom: Why School Reform Has Failed and What Parents Need to Do* (New York: Simon & Schuster, 1996).

15. National Research Council (U.S.). Committee on Increasing High School Students' Engagement and Motivation to Learn. *Engaging Schools: Fostering High School Students' Motivation to Learn.* (National Academics Press, 2003).

16. Herb Childress, "Seventeen Reasons Why Football Is Better Than High School," *Kappan Professional Journal* 79, no. 8 (1998).

17. Don Sabo and Phil Veliz, *Go Out and Play* (New York: Women's Sports Foundation, 2008).

18. Alan H. Schoenfeld, "Looking Toward the 21st Century: Challenges of Educational Theory and Practice," *Educational Researcher* 28, no. 7 (1999): 12.

19. Annette Lareau, *Unequal Childhoods: Class, Race, and Family Life* (Berkeley: University of California Press, 2003).

20. Duncan and Murnane, *Whither Opportunity?*, 4.

21. Lareau, *Unequal Childhoods*, 5.

22. Rothstein, *Class and Schools*, 210; John Haines, "The Creative Spirit in Art and Literature," in *The Nature of Nature*, ed. William H. Shore (Orlando, FL: Harcourt Brace & Co., 1994), 96–101.

Chapter Two

1. K. A. Ericsson, "Recent Advances in Expertise Research: A Commentary on the Contributions to the Special Issue," *Applied Cognitive Psychology* 19, no. 2 (2005): 233–241; K. A. Ericsson and Neil Charness, "Expert Performance," *American Psychologist* 49, no. 8 (1994): 725; A. M. Williams and K. A. Ericsson, "From the Guest Editors: How Do Experts Learn?" *Journal of Sport & Exercise Psychology* 30, no. 6 (2008): 653–662.; K. A. Ericsson, *Development of Professional Expertise: Toward Measurement of Expert Performance and Design of Optimal Learning Environments* (New York: Cambridge University Press, 2009).

2. Daniel Coyle, *The Talent Code: Greatness Isn't Born. It's Grown. Here's How* (New York: Random House, 2010); Matthew Syed, *Bounce: Mozart, Federer, Picasso, Beckham, and the Science of Success* (New York: Harper, 2010); G. Colvin, *Talent Is Overrated: What Really Separates World-Class Performers from Everybody Else* (New York: Portfolio, 2008); Joshua Foer, *Moonwalking with Einstein: The Art and Science of Remembering Everything* (New York: Penguin Press, 2011); Malcolm Gladwell, *Outliers: The Story of Success* (New York: Little, Brown, 2008).

3. E. A. Patall, H. Cooper, and A. B. Allen, "Extending the School Day or School Year: A Systematic Review of Research (1985–2009)," *Review of Educational Research* 80, no. 3 (2010): 401–436.

4. Prescriptive feedback goes well beyond what is typically understood to be reinforcement, which simply rewards success. Prescriptive feedback entails deconstructing what an athlete is doing, often on a biomechanical, physiological, and psychological level, and providing clear direction on how the athlete should change her thinking and behavior to achieve a higher lwevel of performance.

5. Roy F. Baumeister and John Tierney, *Willpower: Rediscovering the Greatest Human Strength* (New York: Penguin Press, 2011), 136.

6. Charles Duhigg, *The Power of Habit: Why We Do What We Do in Life and Business* (New York: Random House, 2012).

7. Ibid., 139–140.

8. Elliot W. Eisner, *The Arts and the Creation of Mind* (New Haven, CT: Yale University Press, 2002), 22–23.

9. Charles A. Murray, *Coming Apart: The State of White America, 1960–2010* (New York: Crown Forum, 2012).

10. David Brooks, "Flood the Zone," *New York Times*, Feb. 7, 2012, A31.

Chapter Three

1. Reed W. Larson, "Toward a Psychology of Positive Youth Development," *American Psychologist* 55, no. 1 (2000): 170.

2. Pete Thamel, "Lacrosse Is Crossing into New Territory," *New York Times*, sec. D, Sports Desk, May 30, 2005.

3. James C. Collins and Jerry I. Porras, *Built to Last: Successful Habits of Visionary Companies* (New York: Harper Business, 1994) , 94

4. J. Lave and E. Wenger, *Situated Learning: Legitimate Peripheral Participation* (New York: Cambridge University Press, 1991).

5. Etienne Wenger, *Communities of Practice: Learning, Meaning, and Identity* (Cambridge, UK, and New York: Cambridge University Press, 1998).

6. J. Lave, "Situating Learning in Communities of Practice," in *Perspectives on Socially Shared Cognition*, eds. L. B. Resnick, J. M. Levine, and S. D. Teasley (Washington, DC: American Psychological Association, 1991), 65.

7. Etienne Wenger, *Communities of Practice: Learning, Meaning, and Identity* (Cambridge, UK, and New York: Cambridge University Press, 1998), 67.

8. Lave, "Situating Learning in Communities of Practice," 63.

9. Wenger, *Communities of Practice*, 263.

10. Hallie Preskill and Rosalie Torres, *Evaluative Inquiry for Learning in Organizations* (Thousand Oaks, CA: Sage, 1999), 11.

11. S. Godin, *Tribes: We Need You to Lead Us* (New York: Portfolio Trade, 2008), 3.

12. R. F. Baumeister and M. R. Leary, "The Need to Belong: Desire for Interpersonal Attachments as a Fundamental Human Motivation," *Psychological Bulletin* 117 (1995): 497–529.

13. Ibid., 497.

Chapter Four

1. Paul Tough, *How Children Succeed: Grit, Curiosity, and the Hidden Power of Character* (Boston: Houghton Mifflin Harcourt, 2012).

2. Ibid., 64.

3. M. E. P. Seligman, *Learned Optimism* (New York: Random House, 1991); Abraham Maslow, *Toward a Psychology of Being* (Princeton, NJ: D. Van Nostrand, 1968); Tough, *How Children Succeed*.

4. Reed W. Larson, "Toward a Psychology of Positive Youth Development," *American Psychologist* 55, no. 1 (2000): 170.

5. Annette Lareau, *Unequal Childhoods: Class, Race, and Family Life* (Berkeley: University of California Press, 2003).

6. C. A. Farrington et al., *Teaching Adolescents to Become Learners. The Role of Noncognitive Factors in Shaping School Performance: A Critical Literature Review* (Chicago: University of Chicago Consortium on Chicago School Research, 2012).

7. Ibid., 5.

8. C. Ames and J. Archer, "Achievement Goals in the Classroom: Students' Learning Strategies and Motivation Processes," *Journal of Educational Psychology* 80, no. 3 (1988): 260–267; Albert Bandura, *Self-Efficacy: The Exercise of Control* (New York: W. H.

Freeman, 1997); A. Bandura and D. H. Schunk, "Cultivating Competence, Self-Efficacy, and Intrinsic Interest Through Proximal Self-Motivation," *Journal of Personality and Social Psychology* 41 (1981): 586–598; T. Z. Keith et al., "Does Parental Involvement Affect Eighth Grade Student Achievement? Structural Analysis of National Data," *School Psychology Review* 22 (1993): 472–494; P. R. Pintrich, "Multiple Goals, Multiple Pathways: The Role of Goal Orientation in Learning and Achievement," *Journal of Educational Psychology* 92, no. 3 (2000): 544–555; D. H. Schunk and A. R. Hanson, "Peer Models: Influence on Children's Self-Efficacy and Achievement," *Journal of Educational Psychology* 77 (1985): 313–322; B. J. Zimmerman, "Self-Regulated Learning and Academic Achievement: An Overview," *Educational Psychologist* 25, no. 1 (1990): 3–17.

9. Farrington et al., *Teaching Adolescents to Become Learners*, 77.

10. Larson, "Toward a Psychology of Positive Youth Development," 170.

11. J. S. Brown, A. Collins, and P. Duguid, "Situated Cognition and the Culture of Learning," *Educational Researcher* 18, no. 1 (1989): 32–42.

12. E. H. Erikson, *Identity: Youth and Crisis* (New York: W. W. Norton, 1968), 968.

13. Michael J. Nakkula and Eric Toshalis, *Understanding Youth: Adolescent Development for Educators* (Cambridge, MA: Harvard Education Press, 2006).

14. Ibid., 6.

15. Ibid., 5.

16. George Farkas, Greg J. Duncan, and Richard J. Murnane, "Middle and High School Skills, Behaviors, Attitudes, and Curriculum Enrollment, and Their Consequences," in *Whither Opportunity: Rising Inequality, Schools, and Children's Life Chances*, eds. Greg J. Duncan and Richard J. Murnane (New York: Russell Sage Foundation, 2011), 75.

17. P. Bourdieu, "Structures and the Habitus," in *Material Culture: Critical Concepts in the Social Sciences*, ed. Victor Buchli (New York: Routledge, 2003), 107–134.

18. Jay MacLeod, *Ain't No Makin' It: Aspirations and Attainment in a Low-Income Neighborhood* (Boulder, CO: Westview, 1995), 15.

19. Anna Badkhen, " 'A Warehouse for the Poor'; Holyoke Absorbs State's Homeless," *Boston Globe*, February 9, 2008.

20. Hazel Markus and Paula Nurius, "Possible Selves," *American Psychologist* 41, no. 9 (1986): 954–969.

21. Carol S. Dweck, *Mindset: The New Psychology of Success* (New York: Ballantine Books, 2008).

22. S. Rimer, "For Girls, It's Be Yourself, and Be Perfect, Too," *New York Times*, April 1, 2007.

23. E. Wenger, *Communities of Practice: Learning, Meaning, and Identity* (Cambridge, UK, and New York: Cambridge University Press, 1999), 73.

Chapter Five

1. Elissa Moses, *The $100 Billion Allowance: Accessing the Global Teen Market* (New York: John Wiley, 2000), 1.

2. Thomas J. Shuell, "Teaching and Learning in the Classroom Context," in *Handbook of Educational Psychology*, eds. David C. Calfee and Robert C. Berliner (New York: Macmillan Library Reference, 1996), 725–764.

3. Richard M. Ryan and Edward L. Deci. "Self-Determination Theory and the Facilitation of Intrinsic Motivation, Social Development, and Well-being." *American Psychologist* 55, no. 1 (2000): 68.

4. Richard Ryan, interview by Gary Taubes, "Richard Ryan on the Many Applications of Self-Determination Theory," ScienceWatch.Com, Thomson Reuters, http://www.sciencewatch.com/inter/aut/2010/10-aug/10augRyan/.

5. Daniel H. Pink, *Drive : The Surprising Truth about What Motivates Us* (New York: Riverhead Books, 2009), 70.

6. Michael J. Nakkula and Eric Toshalis, *Understanding Youth: Adolescent Development for Educators* (Cambridge, MA: Harvard Education Press, 2006), 68.

7. Ernest L. Boyer, "Clarifying the Mission of the American High School," *Educational Leadership* 41, no. 6 (1984): 20–22.

8. Mihaly Csikszentmihalyi and Barbara L. Schneider, *Becoming Adult: How Teenagers Prepare for the World of Work* (New York: Basic Books, 2000).

9. David Elkind, "Egocentrism in Adolescence," *Child Development* 38, no. 4 (1967): 1025–1034.

10. R. Halpern, *The Means to Grow Up: Reinventing Apprenticeship as a Developmental Support in Adolescence* (New York: Taylor & Francis, 2009), 43.

11. Andrew Sum and I. Khatiwada, *The Continued Collapse of the Nation's Teen Summer Job Market: Who Worked in the Summer of 2011?* (Boston: Northeastern University, Center for Labor Market Studies, 2011).

12. Elisabeth Soep and Vivian Chávez, *Drop That Knowledge: Youth Radio Stories* (Berkeley: University of California Press, 2010), 51–52.

13. Ibid., 54–55.

14. Dana L. Mitra, "The Significance of Students: Can Increasing Student Voice in Schools Lead to Gains in Youth Development?" *Teachers College Record* 106, no. 4 (2004): 651; Karen Johnson Pittman et al., *Preventing Problems, Promoting Development, Encouraging Engagement* (Washington, DC: Forum for Youth Investment, 2003).

15. Jeylan T. Mortimer and Michael J. Shanahan, eds., *Handbook of the Life Course* (New York: Kluwer, 2003).

16. Shirley Brice Heath and Milbrey Wallin McLaughlin, *Identity and Inner-City Youth: Beyond Ethnicity and Gender* (New York: Teachers College Press, 1993).

17. Jermaine Ashley, Dawn Samaniego, and Lian Cheun, "How Oakland Turns Its Back on Teens: A Youth Perspective," *Social Justice* 24, no. 3 (1997): 170–176; Milbrey W. McLaughlin, "Community Counts: How Youth Organizations Matter for Youth Development" (Washington, DC: Public Education Network, 2000).

18. C. Taines, "Intervening in Alienation the Outcomes for Urban Youth of Participating in School Activism," *American Educational Research Journal* 49, no. 1 (2012): 53–86.

19. Steven F. Maier and Martin E. Seligman, "Learned Helplessness: Theory and Evidence," *Journal of Experimental Psychology: General* 105, no. 1 (1976): 3; Jean Rudduck, Julia Day, and Gwen Wallace, "Students' Perspectives on School Improvement," *Association for Supervision and Curriculum Development—Yearbook* (1997): 73–91.

20. Michelle Fine, *Framing Dropouts: Notes on the Politics of an Urban Public High School* (Albany, NY: SUNY Press, 1991), 32.

Chapter Six

1. Alex Williams, "And for Sports, Kid, Put Down 'Squash,'" *New York Times*, December 9, 2007, 1.

2. R. D. Putnam, *Bowling Alone: The Collapse and Revival of American Community* (New York: Simon & Schuster, 2001), 18–19; Elizabeth Aries, *Adolescent Behavior: Readings & Interpretations* (New York: McGraw-Hill/Dushkin, 2001), 18–19.

3. M. R. Warren, J. P. Thompson, and S. Saegert, "The Role of Social Capital in Combating Poverty," in *Social Capital and Poor Communities* , eds. M. R. Warren, J. P. Thompson, and S. Saegert (New York: Russell Sage Foundation, 2001), 1–28.

4. Putnam, *Bowling Alone*, 20 .

5. Ibid., 5.

6. Ibid., 20–21.

7. Ibid., 23.

8. Ibid., 25.

9. P. Lichterman, *Elusive Togetherness: Church Groups Trying to Bridge America's Divisions* (Princeton, NJ: Princeton University Press, 2011).

10. Ibid., 11–13.

11. Warren, Thompson, and Saegert, "The Role of Social Capital in Combating Poverty."

12. William Julius Wilson, *When Work Disappears: The World of the New Urban Poor* (New York: Vintage, 1996).

13. Warren, Thompson, and Saegert, "The Role of Social Capital in Combating Poverty," 4.

14. R. Putnam et al., "Using Social Capital to Help Integrate Planning Theory, Research, and Practice: Preface," *Journal of the American Planning Association* 70, no. 2 (2004): 142–192; Putnam, *Bowling Alone*, 93.

15. "MetroLacrosse: Teaching Kids to Stick to their Goals," 2013, http://www.metrolacrosse.com/?page_id=141.

16. P. Bourdieu, "Structures and the Habitus," in *Material Culture: Critical Concepts in the Social Sciences*, ed. Victor Buchli (New York: Routledge, 2003), 107–134.

17. Annette Lareau, *Unequal Childhoods: Class, Race, and Family Life* (Berkeley: University of California Press, 2003), 62.

18. Ibid., 163.

19. Ibid., 244–245.

Chapter Seven

1. David V. Hicks, "Private Lessons," *American Scholar* 66, no. 3 (Summer 1997): 464.

2. Jill H. Larkin, "What Kind of Knowledge Transfers," *Knowing, Learning, and Instruction*, ed. Lauren B. Resnick (Hillsdale, NJ: Lawrence Erlbaum Associates, 1989): 283–305.

3. Betsey Stevenson, "Beyond the Classroom: Using Title IX to Measure the Return to High School Sports"" (NBER working paper 15728, National Bureau of Economic Research, 2010).

4. Ibid., 5.

5. Jack Flynn, "Springfield Excluded from Rising High School Graduation Rate Trend in Massachusetts," *Springfield Republican*, February 10, 2012.

6. S. Danish, V. Nellen, and S. Owens, "Teaching Life Skills Through Sport: Community-Based Programs for Adolescents," in *Exploring Sport and Exercise Psychology*, eds. J. Van Raalte and B. Brewer (Washington: APA Books, 1996), 205–225.

7. Stephen J. Ceci and Ana Ruiz, "Transfer, Abstractness, and Intelligence," in *Transfer on Trial: Intelligence, Cognition, and Instruction*, eds. Douglas K. Detterman and Robert J. Sternberg (Norwood, NJ: Ablex Publishing, 1993), 168–191.

8. Edward L. Thorndike, *Introduction to the Theory of Mental and Social Measurements*, (New York: Teacher's College, Columbia University, 1913).

9. John D. Bransford, Ann L. Brown, and Rodney R. Cocking, *How People Learn* (Washington, DC: National Academy Press, 2000).

10. Hugh Hartshorne and Mark A. May, "1930," *Studies in the Nature of Character* 3 (1928).

11. David N. Perkins and Gavriel Salomon, "Teaching for Transfer," *Educational Leadership* 46 (September 1988): 22–32.

12. R. Halpern, *The Means to Grow Up: Reinventing Apprenticeship as a Developmental Support in Adolescence* (New York: Taylor & Francis, 2009).

13. John D. Bransford and Daniel L. Schwartz, "Rethinking Transfer: A Simple Proposal with Multiple Implications," *Review of Research in Education* 24 (1999): 61–100.

14. Ibid., 62.

15. Ibid. 85.

16. Ibid., 87–88.

17. Susan Harter, "Self and Identity Development," in *At the Threshold: The Developing Adolescent*, eds. S. Shirley Feldman and Glen R. Elliott (Cambridge, MA: Harvard University Press, 1990), 352–387.

18. David N. Perkins and Gavriel Salomon, "Are Cognitive Skills Context-Bound?" *Educational Researcher* 18, no. 1 (1989): 16–25.

19. Steven J. Danish and Thomas P. Gullotta, eds., *Developing Competent Youth and Strong Communities Through After-School Programming* (Washington, DC: CWLA Press, 2000).

Chapter Eight

1. B. Joseph Pine and James H. Gilmore, *The Experience Economy: Work Is Theatre and Every Business a Stage* (Boston: Harvard Business Press, 1999).

2. Ibid., 13.

3. Paul Tough, *Whatever It Takes: Geoffrey Canada's Quest to Change Harlem and America* (Boston: Houghton Mifflin Harcourt, 2008).

4. John Dewey, *Experience and Education* (New York: Macmillan, 1938).

5. Ibid.

6. Jennifer A. Fredricks, Phyllis C. Blumenfeld, and Alison H. Paris, "School Engagement: Potential of the Concept, State of the Evidence," *Review of Educational Research* 74, no. 1 (2004): 59–109; Laurence D. Steinberg, B. Bradford Brown, and Sanford M. Dornbusch, *Beyond the Classroom: Why School Reform Has Failed and What Parents Need to Do* (New York: Simon & Schuster, 1996); Clea A. McNeely, James M. Nonnemaker, and Robert W. Blum, "Promoting School Connectedness: Evidence from the National Longitudinal Study of Adolescent Health," *Journal of School Health* 72, no. 4 (2002): 138.

7. Suzanne Hidi and Judith M. Harackiewicz, "Motivating the Academically Unmotivated: A Critical Issue for the 21st Century," *Review of Educational Research* 70, no. 2 (2000): 151–179.

8. Mihaly Csikszentmihalyi and Reed Larson, *Being Adolescent: Conflict and Growth in the Teenage Years* (New York: Basic Books, 1984).

9. Ibid., 204.

10. John M. Bridgeland, John L. DiIulio Jr., and Karen Burke Morison, *The Silent Epidemic: Perspectives of High School Dropouts* (Washington, DC: Civic Enterprises, 2006).

11. Ibid., 4.

12. David Jordan Shernoff and Deborah Lowe Vandell, "Engagement in After-School Program Activities: Quality of Experience from the Perspective of Participants," *Journal of Youth and Adolescence* 36, no. 7 (2007): 891–903; Deborah Lowe Vandell et al., "Activities, Engagement, and Emotion in After-School Programs (and Elsewhere)," *New Directions for Youth Development* 2005, no. 105 (2005): 121–129; David M. Hansen and Reed W. Larson, "Amplifiers of Developmental and Negative Experiences in Organized Activities: Dosage, Motivation, Lead Roles, and Adult-Youth Ratios," *Journal of Applied Developmental Psychology* 28, no. 4 (2007): 360–374; Joseph L. Mahoney et al., "Organized Activities as Development Contexts for Children and Adolescents," in *Organized Activities as Contexts of Development: Extracurricular Activities, After-School and Community Programs*, ed. Joseph L. Mahoney (Mahwah, NJ: Lawrence Erlbaum Associates, 2005), 3–22.

13. Caroline T. Chauncey and Nancy Walser, eds., *Spotlight on Student Engagement, Motivation, and Achievement*, Harvard Education Letter Spotlight Series, no. 5 (Cambridge, MA: Harvard Education Press, 2009), 1.

14. Judith Rich Harris, *The Nurture Assumption: Why Children Turn Out the Way They Do* (New York: Free Press, 2011).

15. Ibid., 264.

16. Ibid., 264.

17. Malcom Gladwell, "The Coolhunt," *New Yorker,* March 17, 1997.

18. J. Bruner, "Nature and Uses of Immaturity," *American Psychologist* 27, no. 8 (1972): 687.

19. Ibid., 704.

20. Ibid., 703.

21. Ibid., 705.

22. James S. Coleman, "Youth: Transition to Adulthood," *NASSP Bulletin* 58, no. 385 (1974): 4–11.

23. Ibid., 6.

24. Lauren B. Resnick, "The 1987 Presidential Address: Learning in School and Out," *Educational Researcher* 16, no. 9 (1987): 13–54.

25. B. Trilling and C. Fadel, *21st Century Skills: Learning for Life in Our Times,* Vol. 1 (San Francisco: Jossey-Bass, 2009).

26. Thomas L. Friedman, "How to Get a Job," *New York Times,* sec. A, May 29, 2013.

27. "Partnership for 21st Century Skills: Overview," 2013, http://www.p21.org/overview/skills-framework/349.

28. J. Koebler, "Teachers: Don't Overlook Value of Field Trips," *U.S. News and World Report,* December 12, 2011.

29. Reed Larson, Kathrin Walker, and Nickki Pearce, "A Comparison of Youth-Driven and Adult-Driven Youth Programs: Balancing Inputs from Youth and Adults," *Journal of Community Psychology* 33, no. 1 (2005): 57–74; Jacelynne Eccles and Jennifer Appleton Gootman, *Community Programs to Promote Youth Development* (Washington, DC: National Academy Press, 2002).

30. Reed Larson, Kathrin Walker, and Nickki Pearce, "A Comparison of Youth-Driven and Adult-Driven Youth Programs: Balancing Inputs from Youth and Adults," *Journal of Community Psychology* 33, no. 1 (2005): 57–74; Jacquelynne Eccles and Jennifer Appleton Gootman, *Community Programs to Promote Youth Development* (Washington, DC: National Academy Press, 2002).

31. Joseph L. Mahoney and Håkan Stattin, "Leisure Activities and Adolescent Antisocial Behavior: The Role of Structure and Social Context," *Journal of Adolescence* 23, no. 2 (2000): 113–127.

32. Nathaniel R. Riggs and Mark T. Greenberg, "After-School Youth Development Programs: A Developmental-Ecological Model of Current Research," *Clinical Child & Family Psychology Review* 7, no. 3 (2004): 177–190.

33. Floyd D. Jones and Phyllis A. Jones, "Model for Success: The Impact of a Grant Funded Program on an Inner-City Girls' Basketball Program," *Journal of Physical Education, Recreation and Dance* 73, no. 5 (2002); Aida B. Balsano et al., "Patterns of Early Adolescents' Participation in Youth Development Programs Having Positive Youth Development Goals," *Journal of Research on Adolescence* 19, no. 2 (2009): 249–259.

34. Nelson Goodman, *Ways of Worldmaking* (Indianapolis, IN: Hackett Publishing, 1978).

35. Tony Wagner, *The Global Achievement Gap: Why Even Our Best Schools Don't Teach the New Survival Skills Our Children Need—and What We Can Do About It* (New York: Basic Books, 2008).

36. B. Goodwin and K. Miller, "Creativity Requires a Mix of Skills, "*Educational Leadership* 70, no. 5 (2013): 80–83.

37. Kathleen Cushman and the Students of What Kids Can Do, *Fires in the Mind: What Kids Can Tell Us About Motivation and Mastery* (San Francisco: Jossey-Bass, 2010), 2.

38. Ibid., 3.

39. Jim Loehr and Tony Schwartz, *The Power of Full Engagement: Managing Energy, Not Time, Is the Key to High Performance and Renewal* (New York: Free Press, 2003), 133.

40. Marge Piercy, *To Be of Use: Collected Poems* (Garden City, NY: Doubleday, 1973).

41. Ibid., 133.

Appendix D

1. Parker J. Palmer and Megan Scribner, *The Courage to Teach Guide for Reflection and Renewal* (San Francisco: Jossey-Bass, 2007), 104.

2. John Wooden and Steve Jamison, *Coach Wooden's Leadership Game Plan for Success: 12 Lessons for Extraordinary Performance and Personal Excellence* (New York: McGraw-Hill, 2009), 22.

3. Heidi Grant Halvorson, "The Success Myth, " *Wall Street Journal*, sec. At Work, July 24, 2012.

ACKNOWLEDGMENTS

We work at a college as professors. As teachers and researchers, we are accustomed to doing much of our work alone, either in the office or in our classroom. The teaching life—at all levels of education—is a strangely solitary endeavor in that, despite being around people all the time, we have powerful individual influence over how we design and run our classrooms and practices.

Our work in Project Coach has been the converse. The out-of-school world is relentlessly communal and open. Like all the programs we visited, the spaces teem with collaboration, interaction, and a general sense of messy, dynamic give-and-take. For a couple of guys whose lineage tracks back to norms of privatism and isolation, the intense collaboration has been thrilling and ever educative. We have been blessed by the opportunity to learn from so many talented, passionate, and courageous people who have devoted themselves to creating and running programs. In appendix C we provide a list of the many people who spoke with us about the ideas, concepts, and practices that inform this book. The passion and drive of those who work in this field is extraordinary to witness. We learned so much from you.

We wish to extend our sincere thanks to our Project Coach team and to others who have supported us throughout the years. To our Project Coach team: Kym Kendall, who has been with us from our launch. She runs our gyms and has never wavered from her belief that the magic of sport is to build relationships that help young people grow up. To Kayleigh Colombero, our tenacious and huge-hearted director who has been a thought partner for us and for our youth in ways that shape our program and their lives; Dennis Nelson, who helps to run our sports programs and has shared a contagious passion for sport as a social learning endeavor; Andy Wood, our first director, whose vision crafted so many of our core lessons; and Greg Rosnick, whose charisma and understanding of what makes people tick has helped us to bridge more effectively from theory to practice. To our "red shirts," our graduate students who represent our core staff: Darrell Alexander, Will Bangs, Anna Bartolini, Vanessa Bergmann, Kathleen Boucher, Michael Carter, Courtney Centeno, Tricia Chase, Kelly Coder, Elizabeth Colby, Noah Feldman, Kanae Haneishi, Abe Henderson, Emily Hopkins, Mike Kerr, Liam Lattrell, Jake Lauer, Alex Lloyd, Matthew MacKenzie, Dillon McGrew, Joe Martinez, Cristina Masurat, Tom, Messinger, Arianna Miliotis, Elyse Quadrozzi, Matthew Samolewicz, Kuna Tavalin, Marquis Taylor, and Beth Vaughn. To our PC advisory board: Peter Barry, John Gabransky, Mike Intrator, Sharon Siegel, and our new director Jo Glading-DiLorenzo who brings a collaborative spirit to all she does. To Rob Kunzman, a former high school basketball coach who served as a backboard for many ideas. To Alison Overseth, the executive director of PASE and a fierce champion of the out-of-school world.

To our community partners: you opened up your community to us and we learned from you. To Peter Levanos, who welcomed us to his school and helped us launch; to Jimmy Rivera—your love of sport, the North End, and youth inspired us and educated us; to Dr. Jeff Scavron, the embodiment of community medicine, health, and development, who believes that communities like the North End must live healthy, heal, and engage together to reform; to Karen Pohlman, whose understanding of health and community guides us; and to Lydia Martinez, the assistant superintendent of Springfield schools, one of the first principals to welcome us to her school, and a fierce advocate for what young teens can become. Also thank you to the past and current principals who helped us mount the program: Shalimar Colon, Anthony Davila, Diane Gagnon, John Doty, Kristen Hughes, Dr. Stephen Mahoney, and Analida Munera. And thank you to the teachers who have helped us develop our sport-themed children's book curriculum: Lindsay Adams, Brent Anderson, Doug Brunette, Kathy Chamberlain, Ann-Marie Chistolini, Matt Cowles, Caitlin D'Amario, Brian Dutko, Karen Flaherty, and Sean Milbier.

To all the Project Coach teens who have worked with us to create our program, and in particular, to our long-timers who have built the program from the ground up with their energy and ideas: John Cotto, Kiana Figueroa, Effrain Lopez, Ismael Lopez, Loeb Rosario, Tyree Witherspoon, and Joe Wray.

Every writer needs a coach. We were blessed to have Caroline Chauncey on our sideline. Great coaches have depth of expertise, they know how to motivate people, and they see potential and nurture it. Caroline was our coach, and she helped conceptualize and shape the essential structure of our project. As writers attempting to frame some ideas in the field, we had both the gift and the burden of also working as practitioners. Caroline helped us contend with that tension and weave our roles into the narrative of this book. Thanks also to Megan Scribner for helping sharpen our thinking and writing.

Last, to our home teams.

Running Project Coach and writing this book has been a family affair for Sam. His children have played and participated in the program and they have all heard countless stories of the youth and our endeavors. To Kaleigh, Casey, and Riley—thanks for your love of sport and your input and insight into programs like the one we profile in the book. Your ideas and reflections about your own experiences that you shared during dinner conversations or car rides informed the very core of my understanding. To Jake—you have always loved words and writing and now that you're in college, we recruited you to edit and support us in the final stages of writing. I was proud to work alongside of you and appreciated your careful tenacity from a new vantage point. I also still send drafts to my mom, Anna, a retired teacher and my first editor. Finally, to my wife Jo-Anne, who teaches—it's what she does and who she is. It seems like we're always talking about the ideas that animate this book, our program, and our lives. For that I am blessed.

Writing a book is a humbling experience in that it portends that the writers are in some way privy to information and/or understandings about some phenomena that are unique and worthy of sharing. Over the years Don has found inspiration from many folks to engage in such a project, but wishes to convey special thanks to his wife, Sharon, who has spent hours discussing, challenging, and providing extraordinary insights about organizational structures and development, as well as how resources can be acquired and best allocated. Sharon has also provided a remarkable understanding about kids, their needs, and how programs like the ones we write about are critical to helping underserved youth become fully self-actualized adults. However, most of all, he wishes to thank her for the love and understanding she has provided in supporting every aspect of this project.

To our colleagues at Smith College, and in particular, in the Education and Child Study and the Exercise and Sports Studies Department—thank you for the encouragement, ideas, and the willingness to listen.

SAM M. INTRATOR is a professor of education and child study and a member of the Urban Studies Program at Smith College. He has a Ph.D. from Stanford University and master's degree from the Bread Loaf School of English of Middlebury College. Prior to working at Smith, he taught and served as an administrator for twelve years in public schools in Brooklyn, Vermont, and California. At Smith, Intrator teaches courses on urban education, youth development, and the teaching of humanities in K–12 schools. He founded the Smith College Urban Education Initiative—a program that places college students in urban classrooms in an effort to deepen their understanding of the challenges and possibilities of working with youth in urban contexts. Intrator has written or edited five prior books, including *Tuned In and Fired Up: How Teaching Can Inspire Real Learning in the Classroom* (Yale University Press, 2003), which was a finalist for the prestigious Grawemeyer Award in Education. He has received a number of awards, including a Presidential Distinguished Teacher Award by the White Commission on Presidential Scholars, a W. K. Kellogg National Leadership Fellowship, and an Ella Baker Fellowship. He is currently serving as principal of the Smith College Campus Laboratory School.

DON SIEGEL is in his thirty-eighth year as a professor of exercise and sport studies at Smith College, where he helped develop the graduate program that specializes in training college coaches. This nationally acclaimed program has been accredited by the National Council for Accreditation of Coaching Education. He teaches graduate courses in motor learning, sport psychology, and sport philosophy. He also teaches undergraduate courses in sport sociology and in sport as an educational medium for youth development. He has coached on the collegiate and youth levels and was an urban youth sports program consultant for the Boston-based Barr Foundation. Siegel has been instrumental in developing several youth sports initiatives in Boston and Northampton. He has been the editor of Research Works, a section of the *Journal of Physical Education, Recreation and Dance*, has served on the editorial board of the *Journal of Coaching Education*, and has been a reviewer for many refereed journals, including the *Research Quarterly for Exercise and Sport*. He has published widely in the areas of sport psychology, motor learning, exercise physiology, sport sociology, and computing and in professional aspects of sport and physical education.

INDEX